I HOPE WE CHOOSE LOVE

I HOPE WE CHOOSE LOVE

A
TRANS GIRL'S
NOTES FROM THE
END OF THE WORLD

KAI CHENG THOM

ARSENAL PULP PRESS
VANCOUVER

ARSENAL PULP PRESS
Suite 202—211 East Georgia St.
Vancouver, BC V6A 1Z6
Canada
arsenalpulp.com

The publisher gratefully acknowledges the support of the Canada Council for the Arts and the British Columbia Arts Council for its publishing program, and the Government of Canada, and the Government of British Columbia (through the Book Publishing Tax Credit Program), for its publishing activities.

Arsenal Pulp Press acknowledges the xʷməθkʷəy̓əm (Musqueam), Sḵwx̱wú7mesh (Squamish), and səlilwətaɬ (Tsleil-Waututh) Nations, custodians of the traditional, ancestral, and unceded territories where our office is located. We pay respect to their histories, traditions, and continuous living cultures and commit to accountability, respectful relations, and friendship.

"The Chinese Transsexual's Guide to Cheongsam" was first published as "How Wearing the Cheongsam Helped Me Find My Chinese Trans Womanhood" in *Xtra*, October 10, 2017.
"Dear, Dear Life" was first published as "Pursuing Happiness as a Trans Woman of Color" by *BuzzFeed*, October 10, 2015.
"Genie, You're Free: Robin Williams, Mental Health, and the Stories We Tell about Suicide" was first published in *Young(ist)*, September 29, 2014.
"How Neoliberalism is Stealing Trans Liberation" was first published as "Trans Visibility Does Not Equal Trans Liberation" in *them* magazine, March 31, 2018.
"Melting the Ice around #MeToo Stories in the Queer Community" was first published in *Xtra*, February 26, 2019.
"Rediscovering Identity at My Grandfather's Funeral: An Ethnic Trans Story" was first published as "My Mother's Daughter, My Father's Son" in *Xtra*, December 12, 2017.

Cover and text design by Oliver McPartlin
Edited by Shirarose Wilensky
Proofread by Jaiden Dembo

Printed and bound in Canada

Library and Archives Canada Cataloguing in Publication:

Title: I hope we choose love : a trans girl's notes from the end of the world / Kai Cheng Thom.
Names: Thom, Kai Cheng, author.
Identifiers: Canadiana (print) 20190124989 | Canadiana (ebook) 20190124997 | ISBN 9781551527758 (softcover) | ISBN 9781551527765 (HTML)
Subjects: LCSH: Thom, Kai Cheng. | LCSH: Love—Philosophy. | LCSH: Forgiveness. | LCSH: Conduct of life. | CSH: Canadian essays (English)—21st century.
Classification: LCC PS8639.H559 I36 2019 | DDC C814/.6—dc23

Contents

Part 3 LET US BELIEVE

To all the queers who broke my heart
And to all the queers who mended it

Introduction
With Love, From The End Of The World

As I write this book in the spring of 2019, it has become something of a truism among my community of queer people of colour that the end of the world is nigh. A wave of right-wing and openly fascist governments have been elected to power across the world. Wealth and power are increasingly concentrated in the hands of a brazenly corrupt few. Climate change and mass extinction are ravaging the earth, largely unacknowledged by those with the political power to do anything about it.

As for those communities of queer people, racialized people, disabled people marginalized people that have been taking back their power? The social justice activists that raised me to believe in the possibility of a revolution that would change and save the world? Sometimes it seems like the most painful cuts of all come from within my own community: Call-out culture. Lateral violence. Puritanical politics. Intimate partner abuse. Public shaming. We know so much about trauma but so little about how to heal it. What would "community" know about saving us from the apocalypse?

In 2016, I turned twenty-five years old and published my first novel, which was quickly followed by a poetry collection and then a children's book, all to relative success. I became "queer famous" that year. This was also the year that broke my heart, which has kept right on breaking ever since. This was the year that Trump was elected, that millions of people were displaced in the Syrian refugee crisis, and that forty-nine people—most of them queer and brown—were shot to death in a nightclub in Orlando, Florida. In the intervening years, more disasters and atrocities have followed.

My twenty-fifth year of life was also the year that I experienced several devastating personal crises that resulted in the loss of some dear friends and chosen family members, as well as psychological trauma from which

I have not recovered. For all its edgy pretensions, social justice culture had not prepared me for the havoc that abuse, mental illness, and the immense pressure of living as a publicly known trans woman of colour in the social media era could wreak upon my soul.

Not only was I in pain, but my pain was publicly known, scrutinized, gossiped over. People, mostly queer and racialized people, whom I didn't know sent me emails and Facebook messages that were thousands of words long, asking for intimacy and attention and occasionally threatening me when I didn't acquiesce. Journalists asked me for interviews about my private life—my sex life, my family, my mental health; no topic seemed to be off limits. I was stalked, in real life and online. I became terrified and paranoid. I stopped trusting people and this thing we call "community." I stopped trusting myself.

All around me, the people I loved were also in crisis—psychological, financial, medical, interpersonal. When you live in a community of queers, anarchists, and activists, crisis is the baseline and stability an outlier. Among trans women, a life expectancy of thirty-five is the norm.

I lost my faith in community. I lost hope—in social justice, in revolution, in the world.

When we lose faith in the things that matter, it is easy to turn to anger. Anger helps us survive when survival seems impossible. I have been very angry throughout my life, and I still am in some ways. I need to be, to live. Yet anger, and its siblings rage and vengeance, have also been poisonous influences in my communities. I've seen people do awful things to one another in the name of anger and revenge, and it never seems to help anyone in the end.

So in the midst of despair, I have come to believe that love—the feeling of love, the politics of love, the ethics and ideology and embodiment of love—is the only good option in this time of the apocalypse. What else do we have?

I mean love that is kind but also honest. Love that is courageous and relentless and willing to break the rules and smash the system. Love that cares about people more than ideas, that prizes each and every one of us as essential and indispensable. I mean love that is compassionate and accountable. I mean love that confirms and reaffirms us as complex and fallible yet lovable anyway, love that affirms us as human.

I want to live in love and believe in love. If I have to die, I want to die in love. This whole world might be coming to its end, or it might be in the midst of an enormous and terrifying change that leads to something better. Either way, I want to go through it in love with the people I love.

So this is a book is about love, which is a sentence I never thought I would write. This is a book that I never thought I *could* write. It isn't easy to believe in love, not after so many people and ideals I held so dear have hurt me or been taken from me. But, then, I too have hurt people and taken things from people. I have made mistakes, and I have done worse than mistakes. I still want to be believed in, and loved.

So this is a book about love. This is a book about revolutionary love. Love that might not save us at the end of the world but that might make it possible to live through. It may be hard to believe in. It will be harder to live. I hope we choose it anyway.

In love that never dies,
Kai Cheng Thom, April 2019

part 1

LET US LIVE

Righteous Callings
Being Good, Leftist Orthodoxy, and the Social Justice Crisis of Faith

Deep down, I have always believed that I'm a bad person and that the world we live in is an awful place. Maybe that's just what happens when you grow up an effeminate boy (secretly a trans girl) in a Chinese Canadian Christian-ish (not religious enough to go to church but enough to use the threat of eternal damnation as a motivator for household chores) family with class trauma and inherited mental health issues, you know? One of my first memories is of crawling on the kitchen table in our rat-infested house at four years old and thinking to myself, *I'm spoiled. Mommy and Daddy have such hard lives. I wish I weren't so bad. I better work harder.* #migrantkidmentality

Fast-forward to me in a hospital bed in the psych ward, after my suicide attempt at sixteen years old, still thinking the same thing.

DOUBLE fast-forward to me at twenty-six, in 2017, first typing this essay through chronic pain and brain fog in bed on a Saturday morning, STILL thinking the same thing.

So in retrospect, it's easy to see how I got into the whole social justice/radical queer activism thing. Like most of my peers, all I wanted was to be good—or, in the fashionable parlance of various political moments in the past ten years, "rad," "down," or "woke." Like, my mentally ill transsexual ass was never gonna hack my parents' idea of goodness (unlike my Harvard-educated, biodegradable plasticizer–inventing, engaged-to-a-hedge-fund-manager, psychiatry resident older sister), but the *rad queer community* offered me a whole new set of norms for performance and lovability that, at least on the surface, gave value to the identity factors (transsexuality, effeminacy, mental illness, general bad attitude) that had caused me so much childhood shame.

Oh yeah, and I was a crazy trans girl of colour living in a white, cis-dominant society. Where else could I go? What else could I do? It was a whole new chance to be Good, to be Righteous, to Do Good Works and become Lovable at last.

These days, a friend of mine (we're similarly jaded) likes to jokingly/not-so-jokingly call me a "High Priestess of the Movement." Putting it another way, my boyfriend calls me a "microcelebrity." What this means is that I have published two books that are well regarded in the social justice art/activism scene, I'm occasionally stopped on the street by strangers, and I get a lot of likes on Facebook. Also, I get some money for speaking engagements, articles (not this one when it was first published, though), and book royalties (it works out to a tiny fraction of minimum wage, if you break down the money received per hour worked).

In other words, I made it. I'm Good/Rad/Woke™, at least for the moment—all it would take to change that is a few hasty problematic tweets. And all I had to do was incur a mild disability via burnout and post-traumatic stress disorder to get here. Hooray.

Beneath all this cynicism, I hold a genuine curiosity: How did we, the loosely defined social justice left of North America/Turtle Island (one of the original, Indigenous names for this continent) reach this sorry state? I say "we" and not "I" because I think that my personal narrative is illustrative of a general dynamic that a lot of folks in my cohort of social justice warriors (for those new to the discourse, SJWs is the preferred acronym) are experiencing in some form.

There seems to be a wave, if not a sea change, moving through online and RL leftist communities/scenes, a ripple of dis-ease (if you will) with the ways affect (the experience and performance of emotion) and orthodoxy (the creation of norms of political thought and action) are currently playing out. More and more, we are starting to question the ways we relate to politics and to each other.

You can see this ripple being articulated in several pieces of contemporary social justice writing, each of which has been met with some notoriety and controversy. I'm not attesting to the quality or importance, or lack thereof, of these texts. I agree with some of them, disagree with others, and generally feel complicated about all of them. The common thread is their critique of the social justice left from *within* the social justice left:

- Sarah Schulman's book *Conflict Is Not Abuse*, in which Schulman analyzes and critiques what she calls the "overstatement of harm" as an activist tactic that breaks community bonds and reinforces the power of the state to control and imprison people.

- Porpentine Charity Heartscape's essay "Hot Allostatic Load," which is an account of how the author was bullied, exploited, and traumatized by queer scenes that weaponized social media call-outs against her.

- Trent Eady's article "Everything Is Problematic," in which the author draws parallels between student activism during the 2012 Quebec student strike and dogmatic cult thinking.

- Frances Lee's article "Excommunicate Me from the Church of Social Justice," which is a comparison of virtue signalling and shaming dynamics between right-wing Christianity and the social justice left, and an appeal for greater open-mindedness on the left.

- Angela Nagle's book *Kill All Normies*, in which the author argues that the current rise of the alt-right and neo-nationalism in American and, to some extent, global politics was largely inspired by the political polarization of the renewed culture wars between increasingly disenfranchised right-wing Americans and the alienating politics of the American progressive left.

More popularly, the YouTube vlogger Laci Green, a self-identified feminist sex educator who accrued mainstream acclaim and several hundreds of thousands of followers, initiated a subcultural scandal by "taking the red pill" and recanting many of her former progressive political ideas, among them the argument that the male/female sex binary is socially constructed and oppressive to trans people. Green also started hosting "dialogues" with vloggers "across the political spectrum," starting with radical "feminists" who exclude trans women and sex workers from their movement and "anti-SJWs"—otherwise known as the alt-right. On Twitter, Green has decried the *extremely* negative reactions of many of her former fans as regressive, thought-policing, and discursively violent.

I know, right? Blargh! What's up with the social justice crisis of faith? Why is it happening? And what's an overachieving yet politically disenchanted, attachment-traumatized East Asian tranny who wants to survive and also be a decent person in the world supposed to do?

Well, she could write her own essay trying to make sense of it all, for one.

I'm expecting the majority of readers of this essay to be from the social justice movement (why else would you be interested? Are you an anti-SJW/alt-righter trying to use this as fodder for your masturbatory Reddit thread? Ew! Please go away.)

So it will probably come as no surprise to you when I write that, in my experience, there are many leftist and marginalized folks who are not always comfortable with the direction of the social justice left and, in particular, its focus on increasingly fragmented identity politics and the performance of virtue. In fact, most of what I *do* now when I'm hanging out with friends "in the community" is complain about the dynamics of "the community."

Let me pause here to assure you, dear readers, that this essay is not going in an "and NOW I am a classic liberal! Both sides are wrong! I'm not like those *other* progressives" direction. Fuck that noise. I hold the following truths to be self-evident:

- We live in a world fundamentally shaped by the systemic exploitation and abuse of many oppressed peoples.

- Capitalism and ableism are dominant systems of oppression that reduce the worth of individuals to their ability to work and produce goods for the privileged classes. Everyone deserves access to life resources, dignity, and self-determination, regardless of ability.

- For the past several centuries, European capitalism and imperialism have resulted in the ongoing colonization and, in many cases, genocide of Indigenous peoples across the globe, as well as the enslavement and indentured servitude of people of colour. Black and Indigenous peoples particularly have been and continue to be disproportionately targeted for racist exploitation, violence, discrimination, and imprisonment to this day.

- The repression of women and gender-nonconforming individuals, as well as so-called sexual minorities, plays a fundamental role in upholding the structures of oppression at large.

- People who live at the intersections of oppression, such as trans women of colour sex workers, have unique and intensified experiences of marginality.

- TRANS WOMEN ARE WOMEN.

- The work of contemporary movements such as Black Lives Matter and Idle No More is vital and necessary and must be supported.

- Sex work, when chosen freely by the worker, is legitimate work that provides valuable services to the public and should be decriminalized and respected. Sex work differs from human trafficking, which involves the exploitation of individuals' bodies, often for sexual purposes but also for other forms of domestic and manual labour.

• Oppression is rarely, if ever, overthrown through peaceful demonstration alone. Economic and social pressure, as well as direct action and violent protest are all essential parts of revolutionary movements.

So maybe let's just proceed from there, okay?

The mainstream critiques of social justice culture are many, vicious, and largely rooted in either liberal appeals to the status quo ("SJWs are undermining their own cause by being so angry and idealistic! Incremental change FTW!") or outright misogyny, racism, and neo-fascism. I'm not going to bother deconstructing these arguments, mostly because this has already been done rather spectacularly by other thinkers and writers. I'm much more interested in the more complicated "grey area" within the left itself, which is where yours truly spends most of her time these days.

The following list is a summation of struggles I have with social justice culture, while acknowledging that "the community" and "the movement" are not in the least monolithic, or even necessarily a politically united body. I am talking in generalities taken mostly from my experiences of activism and rad queer community in major cities on Turtle Island, as well as from that venerable birthplace of revolutionary thought: the internet. I know that these thoughts are, for the most part, not original. And, undoubtedly, I am oversimplifying certain issues or presenting an unbalanced view of them. My goal here is not to claim the credit for a sparkling new piece of analysis but rather to capture the spirit of my own thoughts and feelings as they have been informed by readings, experiences, and conversations with friends.

And so! Some struggles I (and maybe others) have with the social justice movement's internal culture:

- *Fragmentation of Identity Politics and Essentialism*: In case referring to myself as a "crazy East Asian transsexual" doesn't get this across, I am an Original Identity Politics Girl™. Social justice ideas about identity, particularly race and gender, empowered and liberated me as a teenager and continue to do so today. The language of identity politics allows us to describe social power dynamics that would otherwise remain invisible, such as white privilege, shadeism, and transmisogyny.

However, as resources dwindle and income inequality widens under late-stage capitalism, I think we are seeing increasing fragmentation and oversimplification of identity politics via the Oppression Olympics: harsh competition for resources like funding, attention, and legitimacy, based on the number and type of oppressed identities one can claim. This often happens on an individual level—simply put, in Social Justice Land, we emphasize our marginalized identities and downplay our privileged ones to seem cooler and more important, and to shield ourselves from critique. Online, I sometimes see arguments in which people try to shut each other down using identities as weapons, e.g., "You can't talk to me that way! I'm trans and you're being transphobic!" "Oh, yeah? Well, I'm a femme and you're a masc! Shut your misogynist, femmephobic mouth!"

This type of identity politics is based on a level of essentialism that I am uncomfortable with; it assumes that all people of colour, trans folks, etc., have the same experience, and that identity categories apply uniformly across the board. It also reduces people to a very restricted set of "relevant" identities and erases the rest of their life experiences, while fetishizing the pain of the oppressed. Strategic essentialism—the ability to talk and form groups based on generalities—is an important tool for activism. But the kind of identity politics that discomforts me is not strategic so much as disingenuous and self-serving. It often feels like we are far more interested in diversity of identity rather than diversity of thought.

- *Reliance on Binaries*: With essentialism comes the reductive categorizing of people and systems into false binaries: oppressor/oppressed, survivor/abuser, problematic/pure. Again, these terms are useful in particular moments, but they can also obscure the nuances and fluidity of any one person or situation—as in, how a white, working-class person may in some cases experience more material struggle than, say, an Asian, middle-class person, and vice versa.

- *"Safety" and Regressivism*: The concept of "safety" has come to dominate a particular strain of social justice practices, perhaps most famously the use of trigger or content warnings before discussing or showing potentially distressing material. However, the politics of safety grow more broadly from the movement's emphasis on personal consent—consent to touching, social interaction, and exposure to ideas.

  I am a trauma survivor (*quelle surprise*), and the thought of safety consumes me on a day-to-day basis. I am sympathetic to the need for safety, because most of the time, I don't feel safe. But I struggle with safety politics when the safety of an individual or group comes at the expense of another individual or group's freedom. Alt-righters like to whine about the loss of freedom of speech to the politics of safety, by which they mean white dudes' freedom to be virulently misogynist/racist/transphobic/ableist. I am more concerned about vulnerable individuals who stand to actually lose social access and bodily autonomy. I am thinking, for example, about queer community centres where I have worked that restrict the access of mentally ill trans women and homeless people because their very presence makes middle-class queers feel "unsafe."

  Safety is, I believe, an inherently classed, raced, and gendered experience that frequently runs the risk of being used for regressive ends— ironically, for restricting the freedoms of the vulnerable, those who are never really safe. Often, we see the call for safety actually reinforce the power of oppressive institutions, like the police and the prison system, in our lives. When we choose safety over liberation, our movements fail.

• *Performance of Virtue*: The social justice internet is rife with peer pressure to repeatedly and consistently demonstrate one's adherence to the norms of thought and belief that are currently in fashion. We strive to outdo each other's comments, tweets, and status updates with political critiques and takedowns, while using the latest, most perfect unoppressive terminology. I have heard friends describe this as "activist theatre," where goodness is performed and absolution for the original sins of privilege and ignorance is temporarily granted. Perceived problematicness is frequently ferociously dragged, and meaningful dialogue is rare (though it does occur). The cultural atmosphere is thus more conducive to anxiety-driven attempts to prove one's goodness through faith in the dogma than it is to the creation of authentic relationships in which we are allowed to be imperfect (which is to say, human) or the development of meaningful social change. The performance of virtue often relies on adherence to startlingly simplistic political slogans that are applied rigidly across situations regardless of context. As though wokeness were a factory in which all the same thoughts must be endlessly produced, each just the slightest variation on the one before.

• *Righteousness and Exclusion*: When it goes unchecked, the moralizing paradigm of social justice Discourse (as the kids are callin' it these days) can also lead to a frankly unpleasant tone of superiority and self-righteousness. Those who are not "rad" or "woke" are either considered unworthy of respect or treated as unenlightened potential converts. Frequently, these unworthies are elders or working-class/poor individuals without access to the language of social justice, or people whose cultures hold differing belief systems. Social justice movements, then, become counterproductively centred around white, middle-class, university-educated millennial anglophone North Americans, and those of the rest of us who are able to force our way in.

This issue makes me think about my grandmother, a working-class Chinese woman who moved to Canada in the 1960s while experiencing severe psychosis and speaking no English. She certainly could have benefited from a liberatory movement, but she would never have made it into today's social justice circles as I know them—no one would have understood or tolerated much less helped her.

- *Bullying and Call-Outs*: A lot of public debate has already raged about the benefits and drawbacks of call-out culture in activism, so I won't go too deeply into it. Suffice it to say, a culture in which the majority of political education is done through public shaming is neither all that socially transformative nor psychologically healthy. Call-out culture, in my experience, can also spin into dynamics of punishment through bullying and intimidation, e.g., doxing, online harassment, etc.

- *Celebrityism and Mob Mentality*: In the absence of formal leaders, social justice culture has built a system of microcelebrities (and, in a few cases, not-so-micro-celebrities) from which to take inspiration and direction: artists, academics, prolific users of social media, public speakers, charismatic organizers—and a certain essay-writing, spoken word–performing East Asian transsexual. Such individuals are highly respected among their followers and exert a disproportionate influence on the development of political opinion in the movement—their tweets and posts, writings and videos, are liked, reblogged, and shared extensively as a part of the performance of wokeness in activist theatre. Their names and quotes are invoked like holy texts as a part of the gospel of social justice. They are lionized as living at the cutting edge of activist thought (even though some such mini-celebs are only tangentially, or not at all, connected to actual grassroots activism work), and they are put on a pedestal as living examples of activist purity—of the righteous calling of our movement. In the United States, there is an entire small industry of social justice celebrities who make their living on the speaking/performing tour circuit, funded mostly by student groups with access to college and university department funding.

Yet the standing of such celebrities is also precarious, as the moment inevitably arises when one of them is called out for saying or doing something "problematic"—whether through ignorance or malice, careless thinking/speaking, or a failure to keep up with the shifting landscape of politically correct language. What follows depends on the egregiousness of the offence, the person's social capital, and their adherence to social justice norms of "accountability," a word which here means "the ability and willingness to follow a script for the proper way to apologize." Such a call-out can be devastating to the economic and social security of those who rely on the proceeds of their art, writing, or speaking to survive—usually marginalized trans people and poor people of colour. This makes true accountability elusive, as it is based on personal integrity and genuine willingness to learn, which is hard to achieve when a person's livelihood is under threat

What strikes me as particularly interesting, and disturbing, about celebrity culture in the social justice movement is its relationship to mob mentality and capitalism: We are happy to take political direction from celebrities within the masked hierarchy of the movement, at once elevating and scrutinizing them—that is, until they say something that we do not agree with. The result is an atmosphere where individuals are not encouraged to engage authentically with the complexities and ambiguities of our politics, either because we "are not important enough" or because we have been raised too high to fall. Even more disturbingly, celebrity culture encourages us to view people's value—their right to resources and social inclusion—as contingent on their ability to produce.

• *Critique vs. Compassion*: My final struggle with social justice culture is its tendency to centre critique at the expense of creative thinking. The strengths of social justice ideology are its sharp eyes and tongue, its ability to reveal and tear open the hidden logic of oppressive systems—a powerful and important revolutionary tool. But my fear is that the valorization of critique, and the central role that criticism plays in the performance of goodness, has resulted in rigid thinking that prioritizes the endless re-enactment of outrage and conflict while preventing us from developing strategies for reconciliation, necessary compromise, and collective action.

So there you have it—7 Reasons Why I, an Asian Transsexual, Am Questioning the Social Justice Movement. Too bad I don't work for *Everyday Feminism* anymore so that I could turn this into a viral listicle and get paid seventy-five bucks for twenty-five hours of writing.

You may have noticed, you clever reader, that the struggles I just shared are actually largely unrelated to the "self-evident truths" I listed immediately before them. I am not really arguing against the basic ideology of the movement so much as the ways the movement oversimplifies ideology and creates toxic interpersonal relationships. And yet, as any SJW worth their salt can tell you, personal relationships are the most important political building blocks: *The revolution starts at home.* If you don't have healing relationships, you probably don't have a revolutionary movement.

The problem with leaving a movement, of course, or with rejecting its primary modes of thinking/behaving/relating to people, is that you have to have somewhere else to go. Exile isn't much fun, even when it's self-imposed. And in the current polarized political climate, what with the rise of neo-nationalism and fascism, and the most powerful military state in the world currently being ruled by a narcissistic man-child despot, the only place to go seems to be to the far right (I've been fooled by so-called centrists before, only to realize too late that they were just right-wingers without the backbone to call themselves that).

As for liberalism, that good old ethic of "whatever you do is fine by me as long as it doesn't hurt others"—well, liberalism in its practical form is mostly just an appeal to maintain the status quo, since "hurting others" gets defined as doing anything that upsets the privileged class.

And the problem with the calls that come from such liberals for "freedom of speech," "collegiate debate," and "open dialogue" is that "open dialogue" usually turns out to be a platform for regressives and trolls on the right, rather than an invitation to those whose voices are shut out of both the left and the right. Here, again, I think of women like my grandmother.

This, I think, is how you get a Laci Green—a social justice celebrity with a lot of social capital who experienced some of the relationally unpleasant aspects of the movement—scrutiny, hypercriticism, mob mentality—and then threw up her hands and took a long sliding step to the right. As a pretty, white, young, cisgender woman, she and her desire for "open dialogue" were welcomed with open arms (duh) by the TERFs (trans-exclusionary radical "feminists") and alt-righters of the internet.

Kinda don't think that's gonna happen for me.

So where do we go from here? More selfishly put: Where do *I* go from here?

To those with stable access to "mainstream" communities (read: not the radical left), all this analysis might seem like so much navel-gazing—like maybe I, and all the other snowflakes, should just go and get a life. (Trust me, I've thought about it many times, this Getting-a-Life business).

But here's the thing: I became a High Priestess of the Radical Left not just because I wanted to be Good—it was also because I *needed* to be Good, at least to someone. Needed it so I could get friends and, along with them, access to housing, employment, and health care. I doubt that I would have any of those things, and certainly not at the level that I currently enjoy, without the assistance of the social justice movement networks. Because, you know, I am a transsexual, and without the help of "the community," I am trapped by the untender mercies of the World.

Had I lived all my life in mainstream community—if I had never run away from home, and never found the queer scene—the expectations for my survival would have been to play the part of second-rate woman, to swallow my voice and my needs and perform gratitude in exchange for scraps.

In the social justice movement, the price of a trans woman's presence is to play the part of a revolutionary figurehead, to raise her voice like a Valkyrie leading an army into battle, and to perform survivorhood in exchange for praise.

And my crisis of faith, I suppose, is the realization that maybe I've escaped an iron cage for a softer, more sparkly one. With rhinestones.

When you're a child trapped in a situation of physical or psychological deprivation, you learn shame as an efficient, elegant mechanism of survival: shame simultaneously shields you from the reality that danger is out of your control (since the problem is not that you're unloved and deprived; it's that you're Bad) and prevents you from doing or saying anything challenging that might provoke a threat.

As adults, shame makes us curl away from the intensity and potential danger of authentic, compassionate relationships. It tells us to run away from ambiguity and to either submit or lash out at those who we think might threaten us.

Shame rules community, and not only the social justice kind: in every tight-knit, ideologically steeped community that I have known—Chinese Canadian, Christian, queer—shame and judgment pervade. In the social justice movement, privilege is our original sin, and the doctrine is our Hail Mary. The political workshop and the protest are our church, and the organizers and speakers are our priests. Shame and judgment are the twin faces of trauma, and we are trained to see ourselves and others through their eyes.

And, cynical, crazy East Asian transsexual that I am, I have to believe that another way of seeing, of speaking, of being with one another is possible. That compassion and forgiveness and generosity might join justice and accountability and survival as the core values of our movement. That we might learn to develop tools for reconciliation, even as we hone our tools for battle.

But here's the thing: Dear reader, if you've made it this far, then I have to ask you to think for yourself. To consider the parts of this essay that made sense to you, and to consider also the parts that didn't (you can always throw them out later). A friend once said to me that my words carry extra weight because of my "celebrity status." Well, they shouldn't. I'm no High Priestess; I'm just a fucked-up girl who writes essays in a manic haze.

But I know what I want now.

To paraphrase Emma Goldman:

If I can't dance, then it's not my revolution.

If I can't fuck up and learn from my mistakes, then it's not my revolution.

If I can't disagree with you, then it's not my revolution.

If I can't ask questions, then it's not my revolution.

If I can't decide for myself what tactics I will use, then it's not my revolution.

If I can't be femme, then it's not my revolution.

If I can't choose my own friends, then it's not my revolution.

If I can't bring my family, then it's not my revolution.

If I can't bring my culture, then it's not my revolution.
If I can't bring my ancestors, then it's not my revolution.
And if it's not our revolution, then let's build a new one.

you are allowed to leave

a relationship. a friendship. a partnership. because it is not working out for you. because they are hurting you. because you are afraid of hurting them. because there is no trust. relationships should never be based on fear. should never be based on "they will kill themself if i leave." an adult human life is too much. too much. for any one person to hold. repeat it after me. hold it close to your heart. as you walk away. as you grieve the loss. as you find yourself: leaving is not abuse. getting out is not abuse. freedom is not abuse. freedom is never abuse.

We Need to Confront a Culture of Enabling in Queer Community

Sometimes I worry that queer culture is an enabling culture. Or maybe a more accurate, less confrontational term would be a "validation culture": a culture that places importance on taking individuals' words at face value and honouring their expressed experience (that is, the lived experience they say they are having). There's a lot of good in a culture like that—given that the default in the mainstream/hetero world is generally invalidation, disempowerment, and gaslighting. But I also see the queer validation practices that seem to be the norm in capital-C Community as reactive and unhelpful in a lot of situations.

I was formally trained (some might say indoctrinated) in validation culture as a volunteer in a radical leftist/queer crisis support service when I first entered community as a teenager. Like a lot of queer teenagers, I had seen a lot of crises and trauma in my life without really understanding them, and I was desperate for coping tools. The volunteer training taught me, over a forty-hour series of very intense workshops, that validation in the form of active listening (validating someone's experience unquestioningly, assuming that they always know what is best for them, repeating what they are saying word for word, never being directive or giving an opinion, and saying "mhmmmm" a lot) was the foremost aspect of being a supportive person.

Unfortunately, my training also gave me the impression that validation was the *only* essential aspect of support, and didn't really go into when validation is actually enabling or unhelpful. That there might be other, more complex forms of validation than active listening was also left unexplored. And this approach was politicized, as in, "If you don't validate everything that someone says about their lived experience, then you are Fucked-Up and Gaslighting, and you will harm them for life!"

This is probably somewhat true and can describe well enough the situation of a volunteer who is speaking for brief periods to strangers—playing psychologist and giving half-baked unsolicited advice to people in crisis is generally a bad idea (don't do it!). But the problem is that this politicization of a rigid, specific form of validation seems to be applied to a huge range of informal situations outside of crisis support.

I see this a lot in social justice community in situations of minor conflict, of communal substance use, and of self-harm. In these situations, stress, emotional hurt, and trauma frequently emerge as ingrained patterns—people lash out and intensely escalate conflict, use substances in ways that are dangerous to themselves and others (I believe in harm reduction, but harm reduction is not usually using to the point of incapacitation or acting irresponsibly/violently), and hurt themselves in an effort to manage unbearable pain.

I have seen countless such situations where queers, struggling to be supportive of friends and community members, have adopted validation as the easiest and most politically correct approach. We tell people that they are always right, that their perception of minor conflict as life-threatening is accurate. We tell them that their substance use is fine and their choice, even when it is affecting us or others very negatively. We tell them that they know themselves best, and if self-harm is the only option that they see for survival, then they should go on doing it, no questions asked. In short, we enable.

I don't think we do this because we are bad friends or lazy people (though bad friends and lazy people do exist in community. I have personally been both bad and lazy too many times). I think we do it because this is how queer counterculture has trained us to love. Because so many of our formative experiences of family, education, and health care have been authoritarian "I know what's best for you, and it's for your own good" types of experiences. Because we question the notion that given choices, people will always choose wrong (or that we would automatically know what was wrong for them). And because, often, the immediate feedback we get for providing unquestioning validation is very positive, and we fear conflict.

Ten years later, I am still trying to undo my validation and active listening training—because I want to listen not only actively but also mindfully, compassionately, critically, lovingly. And I want to be listened to in those ways by my friends and family. I have come to believe that support, or at least the kind that comes from loving long-term relationships, is characterized by not only validation but also grounding. Containment. Authenticity. Willingness to enter the space of conflict, as well as the knowledge that we will emerge from it. Sometimes, I want advice from my friends, because the truth is, I don't always know what is best for me. I want to know if my friends think I am doing something wrong.

The part of my lived experience that I express in words very rarely reflects the entire picture of my life. When I say that I am angry and want to attack someone verbally, sometimes what I mean is that I am afraid and want to be safe. In the past, when I have said that I wanted to die, what I meant was that I wanted someone to offer me a way to have a different life.

I believe that in our best, most fallible human moments, the urge to over-validate comes from our fear of crossing boundaries, of replicating the traumas that abusive families and social oppression have enacted on our developing selves. I have come to believe, though, that strong relationships, revolutionary relationships contain the capacity for complexity and tension: That in a loving place, I am able to hear a friend disagree with me and know that they still care for me. That I can receive their advice and know that I don't have to follow it. That there is enough trust between us that our differences will not shatter us.

I don't want to be validated. I want to be loved.

does pain make you valid

does pain make you valid

how integral is suffering to my sense of self?

is pain a precious diamond that i sequester in the chambers of my heart?

do i need twenty-seven names for tears to prove that i know what it means
    to weep?

does tragedy make me interesting and special?

how much overshare does it take to form a trauma bond?

do i need to be in pain to feel like i am living?

would i still make art if i weren't oppressed?

is there such a thing as a pedagogy of the joyous, and if so, where do i find
    it?

Genie, You're Free
Robin Williams, Mental Health, and the Stories We Tell about Suicide

It is a desperate kind of arrogance that leads us to presume to know and judge the reasoning of individuals who have ended their lives. This same desperate arrogance allows for the social illusion that the world we live in is a fundamentally just and orderly place, that the advances of Western science and industry are the solution to virtually any problem, and that everything is under control. By this logic, we are able to minimize the depth of the effect that suicide has on our individual and collective psyches—to label, diagnose, and thus, control the flood of emotions that suicide leaves in its wake.

It is little wonder, then, that when Robin Williams died in November 2014, local and national media networks exploded with all manner of opinion, conjecture, and debate about his much-publicized struggles with mental health. Simultaneously, millions of individuals took to Facebook, Twitter, and other online platforms to post the numbers of suicide hotlines and to blog and reblog articles about mental health while mourning the celebrated actor-comedian.

Indeed, the social media response to Williams's passing reached such fever pitch that some commentators and mental health experts worried about the possibility of "copycat" suicides. This was in response particularly to a tweet by the Academy of Motion Picture Arts and Sciences featuring a still from the 1992 Disney film *Aladdin* with the caption "Genie, you're free" (a reference to Williams's iconic role as the Genie in the lamp).

Most of this discussion, of course, was well intentioned. However, sifting through the outpouring of articles, Facebook statuses, tweets, and comments that inundated my news feeds, I was struck by a feeling of profound discomfort and confusion: the point of all this public discussion of "mental health" was, ostensibly, to mourn and honour one of the most brilliant performing artists of our time, yet the man himself had disappeared. Where did he go? His voice was subsumed by the roar of an audience that consumed him. Like the wishes of the Genie, the meaning of his final choice had been obscured by another, greater agenda: to contain the "suicide contagion" and instead spread the message that suicide is an illness that can be quarantined, constrained, controlled.

To believe some of the media pieces that most powerfully seized hold of the public imagination, it was not Williams but the public who would decide on the cause, meaning, and legacy of his death—as with so many public figures before him. One viral article boldly stated that "Robin Williams didn't die from suicide [but rather from] depression." A writer for *Psychology Today* pronounced him "a functional and productive member of society who chose to commit suicide because of an irrational belief system that convinced him there was no other way to persevere through his emotional anguish." (What relevance Williams's "productivity" in society has to any part of this discourse is unclear.)

Thus, Williams was reduced to a passive victim of mental illness, a psychological statistic (albeit a famous one), an "irrational belief system," a two-line armchair diagnosis. Yet the Robin Williams that two generations of viewers loved was anything but passive—he was a ball of lightning; a crackling, cackling, devilish laugh; a shape-shifting trickster; a ferocious wit. Why, then, did so many of us decide to tell a different story of who he was after he was gone? And why was that story so tempting?

It comes down to, perhaps, the tension between the fantasy that is easy to believe and the complex reality of suicide. It is so much easier, so much less troubling to remove the element of rational choice—to say, as I once learned in a suicide prevention workshop, that "no one ever really chooses to die."

In this way, we can avoid asking the terrifying question of why someone we love might choose to leave us. We can turn away from the possibility that, for some of us, such a choice is less unthinkable than others would like to pretend. But the consequence of this wilful disbelief is the shaming and infantilization of those who are grappling with their reasons for living versus dying.

The intersection of choice and suffering is complex terrain, and the reductionist claim that no one ever chooses to die also implies that it's crazy to want to—that no one "in their right mind" would ever want to stop living. This creates a paradigm in which there are "normal" (non-suicidal) people and "abnormal" (mentally ill) people, with the latter needing to be "cured" and thereby restored to normality. Thus, the perspective on suicide that the person "died of depression" or "died as a result of irrational beliefs" reinforces stigma even while trying to dispel it.

Yet the truth is that most, if not all, people think about suicide and, in my experience as a community worker, usually for many very real reasons that are inextricably linked to individual contexts. That is to say: only Robin Williams will ever know why he died. We dishonour his memory in making our own interpretations, in abusing the fact that the dead cannot speak for themselves.

Williams was the only expert on his own experience, as we are all on ours, and no one else has the right to claim knowledge of his motivations, his emotions, his capacity for logic. Certainly, it is well known that he struggled with substance dependence and depression, but how are we to know whether these struggles were connected to interpersonal difficulties, traumas, or any other life experiences? To simply leap over all of that complicated, messy humanity is to do grave injustice to a man we claim to mourn and respect.

It is so tempting to subscribe to a model that sees depression as an individual illness that can always be cured by therapy and medication— because then, if only we had "gotten to Robin Williams in time," if only he had spoken out about his experience, if only he had been receiving mental health care, then he would not have died. And this may be true in a certain sense. People—all people—do need mental health care of some kind. Many people need psychopharmaceuticals, therapy, and many other types of medical attention. But it is also true that Robin Williams had gone to therapy, and he did speak out publicly about his struggles with addiction and depression. He was a man of means, with access to medical resources. He was much loved, and he still made the choice he did.

We need to ask ourselves: How does labelling depression a physical ailment absolve us as a society of culpability for suicide? How does immediately jumping into a medicalized dialogue around individual mental health allow us to avoid discussing the fact that we have created social environments that make us suicidal? Suicide is always a tragedy, but it is also often a message, a message that points to injustice and suffering in the world that has everything to do with the way we treat each other. When we look at anyone's suicide and say, "That happened because of a mental illness. This person died of illness," we are also saying that person did not die of abuse, of neglect, of isolation, of horrifying individual circumstances, of social oppression, of the fact that just living in this place and this time is very often an incredibly difficult thing.

So let us continue to tell stories about suicide—but instead of seizing the stories of others and imposing on them a preconceived understanding, let us listen to the complexity, the tension, the horrible human messiness that come with them. Let's listen to it all, and accept that we can never fully understand the forces that drive someone to live or die. Let us honour and respect the choices of those struggling, and those who are now beyond struggle—even if those choices took them from us. And let us keep on working, listening, loving, laughing—laughing and loving, above all—in the hope that, someday, no one ever need make those choices again.

if you should start to think forbidden thoughts

if you should start to think forbidden thoughts then come for me

if your bones should start to murmur and hiss
in a language that is not safe to know, then leave

the flickering circle of the village fires
the whispering mouths and darting eyes

leave the books behind as well, the doctrines
the sacred words and unbreakable laws

leave the clustered circle of houses
the barred windows and thrice-locked doors

break the spells they said meant safety, but did not
unravel the knots they said meant love, but did not

and run to the woods where the path is winding
run to the place where the ravenous hide

where the brambles and briars draw blood from your skin
and the branches are as tangled as your hair

lose your memory in that wandering place
give up your body, your promises, your name

remember, child, you were never meant to survive
with your wicked tongue and violent heart

you'll know my house by the scent of cedar fire
and the dolls of clay and bread i've hung from the trees

i will be there, in the centre of the flames
i've been waiting all this time

if you should start to think forbidden thoughts
then come for me

the end of ever after is the beginning of the truth

Stop Letting Trans Girls Kill Ourselves

In 2016, I was approached by community members several times to provide various forms of support and intervention to or around young trans women who were feeling suicidal. This happened to me in both personal and professional capacities. Of course, the professional gets pretty personal when one is a member of the population that one is "working with" in a social service role. In all of these situations, I noticed a recurrent theme articulated by both the suicidal individual and some of the communities surrounding them that frightened and disturbed me: the idea of suicide as an act of personal agency that should be upheld and supported by "the community."

As in, if a trans girl wants to kill herself, and she's thought it through, and she says she sees no other option, and this is what she has decided, then we should not intervene in any way. And if she asks for help in making her suicide plan more effective, less painful, or more aesthetically pleasing, then we should provide that help.

I am not exaggerating.

There are a few different threads of "radical politics" that get tied into this perspective. Consent culture and the politics of body sovereignty are the most obvious. This line of thinking upholds that people have the right to do what they want with their own bodies and health decisions, including self-harm and suicide. If they do not consent to life-preserving intervention, the community does not have the right to interfere.

Woven into this approach are certain strands of mad pride and anti-ableist thinking that critique the power dynamics involved in enforcing saneist, rationalist, and/or institutional perspectives that living is better than death on folks who are suicidal.

And finally, there is a broader critique of suicide intervention philoso-phy/practice as a victim-blaming manifestation of a society that constantly attacks and degrades trans women (and all marginalized people to various degrees), and then medicalizes/shames/further violates them for being suicidal. In this vein, suicidality is framed as a natural, understandable, even politically powerful response to a society that transforms life into a degradation.

The last argument is the one that affects me most viscerally, and in 2014, I went so far as to write and publish an article arguing that society denies vulnerable individuals adequate support, drives them to suicide, and then blames them for their deaths.

I still stand by the sentiment I expressed in that article that suicide is a politically charged, understandable reaction to suffering—both political and personal. But I am now deeply uncertain about the responsibility of having published such a piece in a climate in which suicide among trans women, and queer folks more broadly, is an epidemic that continues to plague us. Every queer or trans youth I have worked with has considered suicide at some point, and the majority have actually planned suicides or attempted them.

I am uncertain—I have regret—because I think underlying all of the apparently political arguments for passively allowing—or in some cases even supporting—the suicides of trans women are powerful aesthetic and emotional undercurrents that reflect our (queer, trans, racialized) communities' trauma histories and deep ambivalence about relationship building and care. I think the idea that we need to support trans women's decisions to die—in other words, *let* them die—comes from the ways we understand and feel about love.

The arguments around body sovereignty and consent are, to me, clearly rooted in a misunderstanding of what it means to provide care (the action of giving help) and caring (the feeling of being cared about). The predominant (white, colonial) queer/trans narrative of "proper" consent to being cared for goes something like this: Someone expresses that they are in pain, or you happen to see that they are. You offer them help. If they refuse, you back off, no questions asked. Any further attempt to help could be considered a violation.

This narrative holds a lot of resonance for me. Both body sovereignty and consent politics come from movements around medical care and sexual/romantic intimacy. But I believe this approach also comes from a traumatized place: it is rooted in queer and trans experiences of abusive families and intimate partnerships in which we were not allowed to refuse, we were not allowed to leave. So our reaction is to swing to the other extreme: we encourage people to leave, and we don't question the refusal of love, even when it is clearly needed.

As a social-worker/psychotherapist-in-training, I was pretty self-righteous and very vocal about enforcing this model of consent/care among my peers. But it broke down when I started to work as a family therapist in a totally non-queer psychiatric hospital setting (the antithesis of anarchist queer community settings).

In my work with families, I often met very young children (as young as four years old) who were extremely angry and emotionally dysregulated because of trauma or other stressors. I mean, so angry that they would damage furniture and physically/sexually harm their peers. These children frequently expressed hatred for themselves, as well as the desire to die. In therapy sessions, they often told their parents that they were going to "run away forever."

More often than not, these parents were concerned and loving but did not know how to respond. They asked me what they should say. From my own place of both clinical training and queer narratives, I suggested they tell their children that it was okay to be angry, that they were allowed to be angry, and if they did indeed run away, they would always have a home to come back to if they wanted. I believed that this was consent, an enactment of the secure attachment—the innate, unshakeable knowledge that one is loved and has a "safe base" to return to—that is so prized in child psychology.

My supervisor (therapist-instructor) agreed with my intervention but also suggested that I had missed an important element: I should also tell these parents to say that if their child ran away, they would go out and find them and bring them home.

The emotional effect this had on me was profound. This was not something I had been taught to believe in queer community—that love and care might mean following someone, even after they have rejected you. That it might mean reaching out, and failing, and then reaching out and failing, again and again.

That abandonment and rejection by a person in pain—child or adult— might be a way for them to find out just how hard someone is going to work to help them not just stay alive but change their life for the better.

This is where the anti-ableist facet of the "support suicide" argument breaks down as well—it may be ableist to dismiss someone's rationale for dying, but it is equally ableist to expect that everyone in a crisis of pain will be able to express or even know their needs in a perfectly linear, logical way. It is ableist to assume that simply asking for consent to intervene once, or even twice, is sufficient to determine whether someone might want or need help.

And in terms of considering trans women's suicides within a trans-misogynist social system, I do not believe that "supporting the agency of suicide" is actually a legitimate refutation of that social system. Rather, it is the ultimate expression of disposability culture. It allows us to disguise inaction in the face of mass suffering and death in a pretense of compassion and radical politics. It is not radical to "support" trans women dying when we are already being murdered regularly. It is not revolutionary to simply accept that society is so terrible that trans girls might as well kill ourselves.

After all, we are the society that surrounds trans girls and sends them these messages about whether life might be worth living. It is our responsibility to change the stakes, to offer different options, to keep reaching out and sending the message that we will never stop trying, never stop caring, never stop loving.

If a trans girl decides to die, that is her decision, and I will not shame or pathologize it. But there is a big fucking difference between not shaming or pathologizing a suicide and being complicit in it.

And the truth is, given even the slightest chance of something changing for the better, I think that most of us would choose to live.

dear goddess

dear goddess
in heaven above
it's me
how are you and how is your wife
the daughter of volcanos
oh, and your twin male lovers
the constellations
are they well
goddess
i know it's been such a long time
since i last wrote
or called
or visited
to be honest, goddess, i
was a little pissed off at you
well, actually, a lot
because of that whole
not showing up thing you did
when i needed you
that one time
with the mirror, and the poison
the bedsheets the razor
that night of the red red stars
goddess, i was so angry
you promised me the world
beautiful dresses gold lipstick
gorgeous poetry
city streets as full and wide

as paradise
and i believed in you
i left home for you
i ran away for you
and then i needed you
and you weren't there.

dear goddess
you broke my heart.

but that was a long time ago
or at least, it feels long
and i think
we can put it behind us
right, goddess?
we were so young
and foolish then
and anyway, if you don't mind
i need to ask you
for something.
goddess, your daughter calls.
by the scent of cigarettes in the night
i call you
by the gasoline rainbows of oil-slick streets
i ask you
by the spilled blood of those gone before
i beg you:
save these young queers
these sharp-edged poets yet unsung
these young

survivors, story-swallowers, bearers of ghosts
give them your love
and bear witness
let the elders speak
as best they can
through the impure vessel
of my body
(all of twenty-six years old)
and let life speak through them
hear my prayer!
save these young queers.
don't let them die
goddess
and don't make me bury them

Part 2
LET US LOVE

Chronicle of a Rape Foretold
Holding Queer Community to Account

When young fags, dykes, and trannies dream of queer community, we dream of a secular yet sacred space: that is to say, we dream of a "safe space," as so many activists are now fond of saying. The queer community that exists in our collective imagination is safe for our bodies, safe for our souls, safe for an infinite rainbow of diverse gender and sexual expression. This is the dream that keeps us alive: the dream of a borderless homeland, a place between places, full of glitter and drag queens and free condoms and magic. In this fabulous, fictional Queerlandia, we are free—free from the oppression of the often violent and neglectful families and communities where we were raised. In Queerlandia, we imagine, no one is exploited or beaten or raped. No one is excluded. No one is ignored. In Queerlandia, our politics are woke and our words are revolutionary. We are free to love ourselves, to love others—to be loved, most crucial of all. Queerlandia is a village, is the Village, in its ideal form. Here, we like to imagine, anything is possible, and nothing bad can happen.

But of course we do not really live in Queerlandia, though real-life Villages and other queer spaces exist aplenty, both physically and on the internet. Real-life queer communities are full of wounded dreamers—how could they not be? And because we are so wounded, we are not prepared for the reality of bad things happening among us—how to talk about it, how to hold it, how to heal from it. We do not know how to have difficult conversations, how to look at each other through the lenses of love and justice at the same time. You either belong in Queerlandia, or you do not. There is no in-between.

Perhaps this is why we so rarely look at ourselves and our own culpability when bad things happen, why we are so eager to brand those who do harm in our communities as monsters. For what is a monster, after all? A creature who comes from the In-Between—in between fantasy and reality, good and evil, healing and hurtful. We make monsters from that which we fear to see in the mirror.

When I was about nineteen years old, I was in love with a gay boy named Cory (not his real name). Cory was white and muscular and beautiful, and because at the time I presented as an effeminate Asian boy (the bottom of the gay male sex hierarchy), I don't believe he noticed my mournful, worshipful love. Perhaps he was just polite enough not to mention it. Cory was in love with another white gay boy, Jonathan (also not his real name).

Cory and Jonathan had an intense, torturous relationship that seemed romantic to me at the time. Their explosive fights and fits of jealousy felt like proof that they really loved each other. In the world I had grown up in, love and rage were so closely linked as to be almost synonymous, and I know that I am not the only one. Isn't that the message that parents give to queer children as they punish them? *Now look what you made me do. This is for your own good. It hurts me more than it hurts you.*

I spent a lot of time with Cory, trying to be a good friend, hoping he would take an interest in me. Instead, he made me his confidante, building the type of one-way support relationship that so many men form with female friends. Listening to Cory talk about his past, his abusive upbringing, his hopes and fears, I realized that he too struggled to distinguish between love and rage. Love and pain. Love and violence. Perhaps someday, I thought with ridiculous naïveté, he would realize we were kindred spirits. And we would heal each other.

One day, I went to meet Cory at his apartment in downtown Montreal after he'd had yet another fight with Jonathan. Perversely, I felt a sort of shameful pride at knowing that I was the first person he called after such conflicts, that only I could provide him with the comfort he wanted. Caregiving has always been my first and strongest language of love, which has often gotten me into trouble. Cory once said that I was very "mothering," and the compliment burned me with humiliation because of its implied asexuality. I didn't want to be someone's mother; I wanted to be their lover.

I arrived at Cory's place and buzzed myself in. I climbed the long winding staircase to his apartment three flights up. The door was unlocked and ajar. The living room was in disarray, furniture overturned and objects strewn across the floor. Cory was weeping in his bedroom. I went in and sat next to him on the bed.

"What's wrong?" I asked. "What happened?"

"Jonathan's cheating on me," he said through tears. "We had a fight. I told him to get out, but he wouldn't go. So I pushed him out, and he ... fell down the stairs."

I didn't say anything. I didn't feel anything either, just a vague, cool detachment, which is what I always feel when terrible things happen. To this day, when I am attacked in the street or I hear someone scream, the first thing I feel is a dead, quiet calm.

Cory turned on me suddenly, his voice raised and shaking. "He was fighting with me too," he said, as if in justification, though I hadn't said a word. "He hurts me all the time, but he just gets away with it because he hurts me emotionally. No one sees how he hurts me. They only see how I hurt him."

Again, I said nothing. I never said anything to Cory about his abusive relationship, though perhaps he knew how I felt. I would not be surprised to discover that he was always more perceptive than I gave him credit for. Our friendship did not last long after that.

If there is any story in this world that I tell right, I want it to be this one. When I was little, lying was the only way I had to survive. In her memoir, *How Poetry Saved My Life*, lesbian poet and sex worker advocate Amber Dawn writes that "lying is the work of those who have been taught that their truths have no value." I have spent my whole adult life in search of the Truth, the kind that you have to tell or die. The kind that you might die telling.

I have been looking for the answer to these questions: *Why do bad things happen? Why do hurt people hurt people? Why do we let them? How can we stop it?* These are questions that we do not ask in Queerlandia. Perhaps this is because if we did, Queerlandia as we know it would cease to exist.

Gabriel García Márquez's classic *Chronicle of a Death Foretold* asks questions of Colombian society that parallel the ones I have been asking. In the novella, a man named Santiago Nasar is murdered by the twin Vicario brothers, who seek to avenge the deflowering of their younger sister, Angela. Neither Angela nor the novella's narrator reveals whether said deflowering is consensual or a rape, but Nasar's guilt for the stated offence is thrown into question by the events of the book.

Written in the form of a murder mystery, *Chronicle of a Death Foretold* bucks genre conventions by revealing the circumstances of Nasar's murder, and the identity of the killers, in the first chapter.

Each of the following chapters explores the events leading up to the murder from the various perspectives of the townspeople. The novella slowly reveals that nearly the entire village is aware of the Vicario brothers' murderous plans but, for various reasons—convenience, notions of honour, fear, laziness, stupidity, and maliciousness—neglect to prevent them from coming to fruition. At times, it even seems as though the Vicario brothers are deliberately boasting of their intentions in the hope that someone will stop them, but no one does. And so, Nasar is violently killed, the brothers are sent to prison, and Angela is left dishonoured for the rest of her life.

Chronicle of a Death Foretold provides a map for the questions I am now asking of the queer communities in which I came of age and in which I continue to live. These are questions about the nature of violence, and about collective responsibility for violence, that are masked by the respective social codes of the fictionalized town in *Chronicle of Death Foretold* and of queer community.

Márquez focuses on the notions of honour and violent death, but I find myself turning in a slightly different, though related direction. In queer community, we already know why our people die: we are killed by homophobia and transphobia, murdered by strangers, family, and a state that seems determined to deny us vital resources such as health care and shelter. What we do not know is why we hurt each other—physically, psychologically, and sexually.

A few years after Cory threw his boyfriend down a flight of stairs, I found myself totally immersed in Montreal's queer punk scene. More than any other city I know, Montreal's queer community is deeply influenced by punk anarchism—a philosophy that reviles authoritarian powers like the nation-state and revels in joyous, unrestrained displays of pleasure and sexuality. In Montreal, to be queer is to be punk is to be feminist is to be anti-colonial is to be sex-and-drug positive (at least in theory). In Montreal, the vision of Queerlandia thrives, gilt-chipped and glittering.

In Montreal's queer community, safety and accountability are discussed in what often feels like an endless loop. Over and over, we affirm the right of every member of the community to live free of intimate partner abuse and violence in all its forms, and we denounce all those who might perpetrate such harms.

Perpetrators, we publicly proclaim, are not welcome at the dance party, the political workshop, the protest, the community service. Names of such perpetrators are circulated via the whisper network, semi-private online documents, and at times, public call-outs on social media. Perpetrators are not welcome in Queerlandia.

But what do we do about individuals who happen to be both survivors and perpetrators?

At that time in my life, I had a friend whom I will call Ronan. Ronan was a boy in his late twenties who, for a time, seemed to have the whole queer scene eating out of the palm of his hand. For one thing, he was beautiful. For another, he was incredibly fun to be around—hilariously funny in the sharp, shade-throwing way that queers love, an amazing dancer, and the absolute life of the party.

I loved Ronan like a brother, and he loved me back, I think because I listened to him even when he wasn't being fun or funny. We went to parties together and we did drugs together and we lay on my rooftop and drank spiked lemonade together in the shimmering heat of the Montreal summer. He told me about his abusive childhood, and I told him about mine.

The one thing about Ronan was that once he got started drinking or doing drugs, he couldn't stop. And when he couldn't stop, he got mean, especially when he didn't get his way. One day, I told him I had to end our hangout because I was going to see my boyfriend. Ronan laughed at me mockingly—and then punched me in the chest, hard enough to make me stumble and gasp.

For a second, I froze, shocked. Then, with the emotionless clarity that I have known all my life in moments when I should be angry or afraid, I slapped Ronan in the face and said, "I love you, but if you hit me again, I swear to God I will hit you back until you stop."

Only now, as I write this, does it occur to me that I once said almost this exact thing to my father when I was sixteen. I wonder if Ronan ever said it to his.

Love and rage. Love and pain. Love and violence. Queers know, better than we ever admit, the relationship between these things. I suppose this is why my relationship with Ronan felt normal.

Violence is normalized in Queerlandia, and so, invisibilized, until suddenly it isn't. Until someone with enough friends and social power stands up and says, "This person hurt me." But most of the time, simply saying that someone hurt you isn't enough to make people believe you. Such is the power of our devotion to protecting the mirage, the glamorous fantasy of our community. We are already so few, and those who would destroy us are many. Life is already so hard, so dangerous. It is easier to turn away, to pretend that we don't see what is happening right in front of us.

In order to be heard and believed, the person speaking about being hurt must use the language of trauma, of crisis, of severe harm. Lesbian author and theorist Sarah Schulman describes this as a process of escalation, in which the suffering of individuals is not taken seriously unless it is articulated in the language of extremes. Schulman states that this can lead to the overstatement of harm, a much-contested hypothesis in queer community.

As a community, we have a tendency to respond only to harm that is extreme and has been explicitly named for us, whereas we ignore the subtler ways in which harm occurs and intensifies. We do not understand how harmful relationships develop or how they progress; we do not recognize the early signs of violence or practise strategies that might help us end it before tragedy or trauma strikes. We do not become actively aware of harmful individuals until after they have already hurt someone so badly that it seems there is no option but to drive them out of community completely.

So we become both avoidant of and obsessed with harm. We try to distance ourselves as much as possible from any hint of violence or hurtful choices. It is unthinkable to conceive of ourselves or those we love as potentially harmful or as having harmed others, because to do so is to lose Queerlandia—which is to say, to lose everything.

Later that year, Ronan and I went out drinking with a group of queers who were famous—in Queerlandia, anyway—as activists and academics. All of them were avowed feminists who regularly spoke and wrote about issues such as consent, queer relationships, and violence.

Ronan's boyfriend, Keith, was a white guy who was one of these famous queer activists. I knew that he and Ronan often had conflicts—Ronan had grown up poor and racialized, and Keith had grown up white and very rich. There were bound to be conflicts, rooted in an imbalance of social and financial power, that Ronan railed against. I supported Ronan in this, because I knew what it meant to be the more marginalized, the *lesser* member of a partnership.

That night, Ronan and his boyfriend had a fight. Like most fights with Ronan, things started slow, and then suddenly exploded. Through the streets of Montreal's North End they argued, until without warning, Ronan lost his temper completely and slammed his fist into Keith's face. I heard the impact, heard the air burst out of Keith's lungs. I saw his eyes widen, his face flush, the blood spray from his mouth and land in droplets on the pavement, black under the streetlamps.

Thoughts of Cory and Jonathan rushed through my head. I had promised myself that the next time I saw intimate partner violence, I would do something about it. And, besides, this time I wasn't alone—I was surrounded by famous queer activists, for God's sake, all of them almost a decade older and more experienced than me. They would know what to do, I thought.

But no one did a thing.

Sometime later, I asked one of the famous queer activists what he thought of that night.

"I don't think that what Ronan did is okay," I said.

He looked at the floor. Heaved a sigh. "Yeah," he said, "I just try not to think about it."

When I first entered queer community, I was taught that it is always the perpetrator rather than the survivor who is responsible for an act of intimate violence. This message, drilled into me over and over by the people I trusted, forms a core component of the belief system of the queer communities I am a part of. I still believe it to be true, on one level. On another, I wonder if there are other truths that we miss when we focus solely on understanding intimate violence as an individual choice made by a few monstrous people, rather than as part of a systemic problem in which we all play a part.

Let me be clear: survivors of sexual assault and intimate violence are never responsible for the actions of the person or people who have harmed them. What I am suggesting is that it is important to examine the ways in which communities create and actively maintain the conditions in which such violations are likely to occur. Reacting punitively is not a means of preventing harm.

Queerlandia is full of doublespeak and contradiction, because it is a dream created by humans. We long for safety and order, but we love the thrill of transgression and danger. We are obsessed with sex and claim to be sex positive, but we are terrified of its potential for hurt.

In queer community, I was told that consent was sacred above all things, and then repeatedly thrown into situations crowded with people who were drunk or high beyond all capacity for consensual communication. The very people who taught me in workshops and pontificated on social media about the importance of consent touched and grabbed and kissed me repeatedly without ever asking what I wanted.

We claim to create safer spaces to express sexuality, but we have no idea how to actually do this. A party cannot promote healthy sexuality simply by placing a sign at the entrance that says, *RAPISTS NOT WELCOME*. A community cannot teach consensual intimacy by ignoring violent behaviours until someone stand and screams, "THIS PERSON SEXUALLY ASSAULTED ME," and then summarily exiling the accused.

Beneath the mirage of Queerlandia, there are real people, real places, full of anger and pain. We carry the memories of trauma we have survived in our families of origin, in a transphobic and homophobic society, and we re-enact them on each other's flesh.

As a young person just entering Queerlandia in my late teens and early twenties, I relied on those I considered to be elders and mentors, most of whom were perhaps only ten years older than me, or less. But I was deeply vulnerable, and needy, largely because my parents were not capable of giving me the guidance I needed as a trans woman of colour growing up in a homophobic and transphobic migrant community. I needed queer people, trans people to teach me about queer norms, queer culture, queer sex. I needed queer people to teach me what I needed to know, to protect me.

The mentorships I had were mostly informal, and their boundaries were never explicitly discussed. Some mentors were generous, and for this I will always be grateful, but no one ever actually said, "I am a safe adult for you, and here is what that means. This is what I can give you, and this is what I cannot." Perhaps because of this, I had no idea what to expect from a mentor, no idea what was appropriate and what wasn't.

Where were the elders of Queerlandia when I was being abused? Why didn't they say anything, do anything? Why didn't they protect me? Who takes the responsibility for parenting and leading a community where almost all of us are children who have been forced to flee our parents?

In her poetry, Leah Lakshmi Piepzna-Samarasinha asks the question, "What kind of elder do you want to be?" It's a question that haunts me. I know what I wanted from an elder. Guidance. Connection. Teaching. I wonder if I know how to give these things to another person. I look at the young people in my life and see how intense their longing is. It is a longing that mirrors my own. How do you become an elder when you barely had any yourself? In community, we romanticize our elders, but we have little idea of what generational responsibility actually entails, or how to form intergenerational relationships grounded in both intention and integrity.

If I had received true intergenerational guidance in Queerlandia—if I had been taught and cared for by mentors who were looking out for my best interests—would rape, sexual assault, and exploitation still have happened to me?

Something I have wondered for a long time now is why my own experiences of living through violence within queer community went unnoticed for so long—unnoticed by community and disregarded by myself. It is in part, I imagine, because of my own inability to articulate the abuse as such. No one named the abuse that was happening to me, so no one knew it was happening—even when it was right in front of us.

This is why, I think, it was possible for a queer man that I had never met before to come up behind me at a party in one of Montreal's punk bars, grab me with both hands, and start slamming me repeatedly against a wall.

No one said anything. No one did anything. No one came to help me, to try to pull this person off of me. No one moved as I fought to breathe, as my bones screamed against the unyielding surface of the wall, as I grabbed at his arms and finally threw him off me. No one responded when I ran outside and said to the small crowd of people taking a smoking break, "Hey, that guy in there just attacked me!"

These weren't people I didn't know. They weren't some random straight people on the street watching a trans woman get attacked and beaten up by a homophobe. They were community members, friends of mine, doing nothing while one of their friends attacked me in a way that could have caused permanent bodily harm. I still remember who was there, all of their names.

Years later, I still get angry, still feel the rush of heat prickling down my spine, as I think about it. Why didn't they move? Why didn't they care? Why didn't anyone ask me if I was okay? Was it because the attack wasn't obviously sexual in a way that we tend to understand sexual assault? Is potentially deadly physical assault less heinous in the eyes of queer community? Or did it just not matter because it was me who was assaulted? Or was it because

I was not white, not yet a published writer, not yet "important" that this assault was unworthy of response?

Over the years, I've watched some of these queers make public call-outs demanding their abusers be kicked out of community. Sometimes, they got what they wanted, on the strength of the assertion that we should always believe survivors. But these same queers saw what happened to me at that party with their own eyes, and they couldn't be bothered to help me.

Why did their pain matter more than mine?

I had intended, at this point in the essay, to include an illustrative anecdote of my own experience of sexual violence. That seems the thing I ought to do. I had meant for this essay to centre my experience of abuse as a metaphor for the larger problem of intimate violence in queer community—that is to say, a problem that is known by all but directly addressed by few. We know that violence is happening, we see it in progress, we can even predict, to some extent, who is going to be harmed, yet we do very little about it—though we speak a lot.

But my experience of abuse is not a metaphor. My body is not a metaphor. My life is not a metaphor.

Survivorhood should not function as some sort of ticket to enter into the public discussion of intimate violence. We should not have to say the words "I have been raped" to be taken seriously, nor should we have to list the names of the people who have hurt us to receive support.

We live in a rape culture, as feminists like to say, queer community included. What this means, at least for trans women of colour like me—targets of violence who are among the least likely to be supported as survivors—is that our perpetrators are not limited to one bad person, or two. My intimate life—both sexual and non-sexual—has in large part existed on a spectrum of violence that encompasses the majority of my sexual partners and many of my friends.

The problem of intimate and sexual violence is not individual; it is cultural. That is to say, we are responsible for it. All of us. You are.

Me too.

What would it take to build a community where we were really safe? Not perfectly, rigidly safe in the sense of totally free from risk—because such a thing is not possible in this life—but safe enough to pursue intimacy and adventure with the knowledge that there really was a community that had our backs? Where we were safe enough to make mistakes, to hurt people in the way that all of us sometimes do, through carelessness or clumsiness or plain stupidity, and to make amends in a way that created healing instead of more hurt? Where the rape and traumatization of trans women of colour was not a foregone conclusion?

I think it would mean giving up the dream of Queerlandia, a dream that has kept us alive, true, but has also entrapped us, like spiders caught in our own dystopian webs. For Queerlandia is a dream of perfection, which means that only perfect people—perfect victims, perfect survivors—can live there. Perhaps this is why so many of the queer community members I know who speak the loudest about violence and the need to ostracize perpetrators are also frequently those whom I have witnessed bullying others, pursuing non-consensual intimacy, and engaging in psychological manipulation.

What if instead of waiting for a toxic relationship between two queer community members to explode into the cycle of call-outs and ostracization that so many of us know all too well, we actually spoke to each other and intervened when we saw that one or both members seemed to need help? What if we were not afraid to ask the question "I'm sorry if I am totally wrong and this is none of my business, but is it possible that your relationship is hurting you?"

What if we organized our scenes and communities into groups of chosen family, each of which had access to mentorship from elders, so that when a close friend or lover committed an act of harm, we were ready to hold them accountable in a non-punitive and loving way?

What if instead of hunting for the monsters who live among us, we took a long and loving, courageous look in the mirror? Who might we see then?

Queerlandia is the place that I longed to live in when I was a child growing up in an abusive environment. Queerlandia is what I imagined, fought for, was ready to die for. Queerlandia saved my life by giving me a reason to live. It is fantasy, revolutionary vision, hard and glittering and surprisingly sharp, like a drag queen's shoes. It is only the shell of perfection, the illusion of safety painted over the surface of a more desperate reality.

I want to live in the real world now—an uglier place, to be sure, but I hope, a more honest one. I have spent my entire adult life searching for the Truth. It's possible that I've been looking in all the wrong places.

how many times?

how many times
has queer community
broken your heart?

how many times
would you let a lover break you
before you walked away?

how has queer community
loved you?

Complications of Consent

Like many people, I struggled with the giant social media trigger fest that the #MeToo movement sparked. Beginning in fall 2017, for more than a year, every day, we were inundated with this story and that opinion piece—and still, in 2019, they keep coming, though at a somewhat reduced rate. And I keep seeing people from all over the political spectrum conspicuously chest-beating about the terrible times we live in.

We should believe and support people who have been raped and abused; this is the lesson that #MeToo is finally imparting in its painful way. We are entering a time when power dynamics in sex are rightly being questioned—for example, we are beginning a long-overdue examination of the power dynamics in sexual relationships between professors and their students, and between older adults and younger adults. But one of the hardest things for me about #MeToo is seeing "social justice activists" and "feminists" of all genders loudly proclaiming how much they know about sexual consent and how good and consensual their sex is and how terrible everyone else is who doesn't know as much as they do. I have dated some of these folks, and worked and shared space with others, and I know firsthand that their consent practices could use some help. Similarly, my own consent practices have really needed improvement, and they will continue to need to be amended throughout my life.

This is just one tiny piece of a giant conversation that society needs to have about sex, consent, and violence in contemporary culture. Liberal consent culture has failed us, having been co-opted by the prison-industrial complex and white feminism. Punitive justice models like those offered by the prison system and supported by mainstream white feminism have given us the spectacle of trials (both legal and in the court of public opinion), but they have not offered us healing or a way forward.

We actually don't really know what we are talking about when it comes to consent. And we do everyone a disservice when we claim that we all share the same definition of consent, that consent is easy to define or practise, or that the liberal standard of consent as "explicit (i.e., verbal), informed, ongoing, and enthusiastic" is applicable to everyone in all situations.

We have entered a resurgence of the second-wave feminist sex wars, in which the classic debate over sexual liberty versus sexual safety has been revived. The term "sex positivity" gets thrown around a lot in third-wave feminism, yet the majority of us don't seem to have a strong grasp of how to practise positivity toward sex that does not fit the heteronormative model of romance between two people who know everything about each other, absolutely love the sex that they have 100 percent of the time, and communicate perfectly, without any power dynamic issues.

There is a pernicious strain of sex negativity that pervades liberal consent culture—the kind of consent culture that is deployed on college campuses and in non-profit organizations. Consent culture taught me what rape was a thousand times but never showed me how to have sex in a way that was actually accessible to me. Consent culture, for me, took the form of a gay white boy lecturing me for making a "rapey" joke about groping guys on the dance floor when they were already groping me. That same gay white boy enjoyed licking me whenever he felt like it, without asking, despite my protests.

Consent culture teaches us that all sex exists in a binary—good and consensual (explicit, ongoing, informed, and enthusiastic) versus rape, where rape is understood to be the vilest and evilest of all sins and the most traumatic experience anyone could ever have. This perspective on rape becomes the only way of looking at sex that is unenjoyable or painful. Many situations, however, are more ambiguous than this.

The idea that any sex that is unwanted or unenjoyable (and thus not enthusiastic) is rape is fuel for the paternalistic "trafficking" narrative of whorephobia, since sex workers supposedly cannot decide for themselves what kind of sex they want to have, when, and for what reasons.

The definition of consent as "explicit, informed, ongoing, and enthusiastic" has been used to undermine the rights of sex workers, HIV-positive people and others with STIs, disabled people, and trans people for a long time. Many national governments are using the notion of "informed" consent to criminalize and jail HIV-positive people for not disclosing sensitive health information to partners, whereas we know that doing so can result in physical and systemic violence. "Informed" consent has also been used as a justification for the murder of trans women who do not disclose their assigned gender to their partners, for the very reason that doing so can result in being killed, as in the historic case of Gwen Araujo. Notably, there is a faction of cis lesbian-identified feminists who claim that trans women not disclosing their trans status to romantic partners, even before any sex has occurred, is akin to rape.

On an individual level, most of us have participated in sex without "explicit, informed, ongoing, and enthusiastic" consent for the simple reason that human interactions are not usually like this—most certainly not ones as emotionally charged and physically engaged as sex.

As a young person who had mental health struggles but who also deeply desired and feared sex, I often placed myself in risky sexual situations where communication and power dynamics were unclear. Some of my partners were similarly vulnerable to me, but many were older, more experienced, wealthier, physically stronger. I often consented verbally to sex that was painful (not enjoyable), that felt confusing or exploitative, because I wanted to feel loved or sexy. Sometimes I was high or drunk, and sometimes my partners were too. In the space of a single encounter, I could experience pain, pleasure, confusion, connection, mentorship, and violation.

Did I deserve better? Absolutely. Were my partners capable of giving me better (as in, did they have the perspective, the experience, the knowledge)?

Sometimes, but not always. Did I sometimes hurt others? Yes, though never through force or manipulation. My mistakes, like most of my peers', were in not knowing what boundaries were. I had never been taught that I had boundaries at all.

So I wasn't always safe when I had sex. And sometimes I wasn't totally safe to be with when I had sex. It's terrifying to say that in this political climate of intense shame and scrutiny around sexual behaviour, but maybe that's why it must be said. I don't always know what to make of that. But I also know that I am far from alone—that the majority of queer people have experienced sex like this, at many ages.

Still, I had agency. Still, I had a right to my sexuality. This, I believe, is a messier and truer kind of sex positivity—holding all these truths at once while believing in human goodness and the possibility of healing and growth, the possibility of pleasure that comes from experience.

Liberal consent culture taught me to see myself as a victim in a hundred different ways but never helped me find my power outside of victimhood.

I have been raped and abused. But I should not have to say that, to use those words, that story that someone else has written, in order to be believed that I have been hurt. That I am in pain. That some of the things that happened to me were wrong. I deserve that space, that room for my agency and humanity. We all do.

boundaries i

boundaries
are not about yes
or no
they are not about limitations
or permission or even
this thing we call consent
they are the space
between *me* and *you*
the borderland
where fear ends
and desire begins
they are the place
where love can live
without being lost

Melting the Ice around #MeToo
Stories in Queer Community

As the mainstream #MeToo movement that began in 2017 continues to name abusers and attempt to hold them accountable into 2019, #MeToo accusations are also still taking place in queer community; for example, the sexual assault allegations made against famed Hollywood director Bryan Singer, whose blockbuster films include *X-Men* and the Oscar-nominated *Bohemian Rhapsody*. The accusations against Singer echo previous stories about gay actors Kevin Spacey and George Takei, the latter of whom turned out to be innocent. Then, there were the sexual harassment claims against the *Transparent* TV show actor Jeffrey Tambor, and the silence in response to the allegations from the show's creator, Jill Soloway.

I felt strangely—inappropriately—disaffected, almost bored, when I started to write this essay, which was originally commissioned by *Xtra* as an op-ed on queer #MeToo stories in light of recent events in Hollywood, chief among them the news about Singer. The implication, I suppose, was that queer community is long overdue for its own reckoning around sexual abuse and assault, and Singer and Spacey seem to be living proof of that. However, it doesn't seem as though there has been any lack of discussion about queers and sexual violence in the recent past. A quick Google search of the combined terms "queer" and "#MeToo" brings up several pages of articles and think pieces about sexual violence and LGBTQ2 folks—ranging in scope from the erasure of trans women from #MeToo discourse to the prevalence of rape culture among gay men.

Indeed, sometimes it seems that my entire adult life as a queer person has been inflected by furious discussion about the presence of sexual abusers among us—so much so that I often feel disturbingly desensitized to it. From the perspective of a community member, I can attest that public call-outs of queer perpetrators of sexual violence have been going on since long before the mainstream, heterosexual #MeToo moment began. These call-outs have had varying impacts on queer people's actual lives, often failing to set boundaries on the behaviour of privileged abusers, whereas severely impeding the lives of extremely marginalized individuals.

I recall seeing an extremely popular white, cis gay man called out for rape on Facebook and suffer relatively few apparent consequences: he stayed on social media, continued to regularly attend queer events, and ran a successful community business. I also recall seeing a trans woman of colour called out for emotional manipulation of her romantic partner. This trans woman was summarily banished from the city's queer spaces, kinship networks, and social events. She developed what appeared to be intense paranoia and eventually vanished from social media. I have no idea what happened to her.

Queer community doesn't lack for discourse around sexual abuse. On the contrary, we are steeped in it, and have been for some time. Yet for all our talk, not much seems to have changed—there are still victims, and there are still abusers.

This raises some interesting questions: What do we really need to say to each other about sexual abuse and queer community? What truths, and whose stories, are getting lost beneath the primal scream that is our collective pain?

Trauma theory and its quest to understand the survival mechanisms of the human body may hold some answers. As a former therapist, I have learned that the sensation of boredom, of emotional detachment in response to stressful stimuli is a subtle form of traumatic response: The human brain seeks to protect itself with not only the instinctive fight-or-flight responses that we are used to seeing in trauma survivors but also the freeze response.

The freeze response is characterized by involuntary emotional numbing. It is an ancient, brilliant defence mechanism, particularly in situations where danger is ongoing, repeated, and unlikely to be overcome by fighting or fleeing. For example, when experiencing a sexual assault, many survivors will undergo a sort of psychological paralysis in which the processes of thinking and feeling instinctively shut down to protect the survivor from further harm.

Individuals who live in highly traumatizing environments, such as high-conflict areas or abusive families, might experience freeze as their emotional baseline, punctuated by fight-or-flight moments of intense, brief crisis. Such individuals may have a difficult time connecting to strong emotions, such as fear, anger, or sadness, and will often instead feel empty and disconnected from others.

What does the freeze response have to tell us about the untold stories of sexual violence in the queer community? For starters, it might help to explain the peculiar and ferociously charged dynamics around secrecy, disclosure, and punishment that characterize our community's discussions and understandings of what constitutes sexual violence between people.

For a community that is supposedly steeped in progressive politics, sex positivity, and mutual love, queers hurt each other—horribly—an awful lot. Nearly half of individuals who identify as gay or lesbian report experiencing sexual violence or psychological abuse from a partner, and more than half of bisexual individuals experienced the same. Similarly, more than half of trans people report having experienced intimate partner violence in their lifetime. And trans feminine individuals, particularly those of colour, are much more likely than other groups to experience physical violence and be murdered by their partners.

This creates the perfect environment for a collective freeze response, a community-wide numbing of the soul. Queer community, for all its beauty and strength, is also a closed environment, in which sexual violence is pervasive and ongoing. This violence renders itself invisible, not by hiding but by being everywhere at once: bathhouse culture, party culture, queer sex culture. We all see it, but we become numb to it; it feels banal. What's the point of talking about it? Nothing will change. Having hard conversations can only hurt us.

This numbness persists until it bursts free in moments of intense, furious crisis, erupting into fight-or-flight responses that take the form of call-outs, social shunning, "cancelling," exile. These strategies serve a powerful emotional role in small communities, especially those traumatized and underserved by traditional law enforcement. After all, we want and deserve to feel safe. Sometimes, also, we want revenge against those who have hurt us—and it isn't wrong to want revenge when we have been abused.

But community responses to abuse that are grounded in ostracization and social shaming do not work. Fight, flight, and freeze are excellent responses to trauma when it comes to individual, momentary survival, but we pay a price for them in human connection. When we rush to punish wrongdoers through social mobbing and exclusion, we lose the opportunity to understand the root causes of harm and thereby prevent it in the future. We also run the risk of perpetuating an imbalanced penal system in which only the vulnerable are punished—like the trans woman of colour I knew who was called out and banished from queer community.

Models of justice that centre punishment do not prevent abuse but only react to it, and they don't offer a pathway toward healing for either perpetrators or survivors. Nor do they acknowledge the dual reality that a great many perpetrators are themselves survivors. A 2019 study at McMaster University by researcher Claire Bodkin, published in the *American Journal of Public Health*, shows us that approximately half of prison inmates have experienced abuse in childhood.

Sometimes I wonder: If we exiled every single queer person who had ever done anything sexually inappropriate, abusive, or violent, would there be a queer community left?

In a society built on rape culture, settler colonialism, and capitalism, sexual assault and harassment narratives are frequently assigned negative value. They are always loaded with the power to harm both the speaker and the listeners but only very rarely the power to spark healing in anyone. Small communities, such as the queer community, suffer particularly from this paradigm that centres punishment rather than healing. We are already so often at war with the external world. To speak up against abuse—even among our communities—is to bring war inside our own fortress. In a 2019 article in *GUTS* magazine called "A Conversation I Can't Have Yet: Why I Will Not Name My Indigenous Abusers," Indigenous trans femme poet and performer jaye simpson describes this dilemma in the context of the Indigenous community. "Why not just name these men and women and state publicly how they harmed me? Simply, because they are Indigenous," simpson writes. "More complicatedly, because the justice system would misgender me and I was threatened with court if I did. More seriously, because one of us would end up dead."

How do you call out the community that took you in when your family wouldn't? How do you call out the people who loved you, whom you still love? The people who taught you who you were and helped you to survive? How do you call out your lovers, friends, mentors, role models when you're not sure either of you will survive?

Sometimes the only safe thing to do is to be silent. To freeze.

The #MeToo movement is like a sudden surge in global temperature that melts the layer of ice covering the planet: old things, buried things, suddenly rise to the surface and burst open in all their toxicity. Society's collective freeze response, which manifests as silence and looking the other way, suddenly gives way to fight—a burst of righteous rage, recrimination, punishment. In 2019, R. Kelly is newly infamous for his sexual abuse of young Black women. Yet it was the opposite of a secret that he had sexual relations with the singer Aaliyah when she was fifteen and he was twenty-seven, and then married her openly, in 1994. Although Aaliyah later had the marriage annulled and its records expunged, it was her career, not Kelly's, that suffered. For all the people who are now ferociously decrying Kelly, a single question comes to mind: Where were you then?

We might ask this same question of all the Hollywood film industry professionals who supported Woody Allen for decades, who lauded and participated in Roman Polanski's artistic projects, despite the accusations of sexual assault levelled against them, and who are now supposedly staunch supporters of #MeToo. Meanwhile, on a social plane far below that of American cinema elites, queer community is struggling with similar questions on a smaller scale—when our first response to horrible abuse is to freeze and remain silent, how do we go back and make things right? How do we face our own hypocrisy, our own complicity?

Trans woman writer and video game maker Porpentine Charity Heartscape writes about disposability culture in her polemic "Hot Allostatic Load," observing bitterly that communities truly punish only those whom it can do without—those who have suddenly become expendable, or who have always been. Heartscape writes, "Punishment is not something that happens to bad people. It happens to those who cannot stop it from happening. It is laundered pain, not a balancing of scales." This line has always, will always, haunt me.

Perhaps this is why it sometimes feels like we are always talking about accountability for abuse in queer community while also never talking about it: For a long time, we have only been talking about accountability for some people and not for others. We purge our pain on mentally ill trans femmes and queer people of colour to spare our favourite white queer celebrities and organizers, the same way that Hollywood spared Allen and Polanski.

Although the recent move to hold accountable powerful abusers—Allen, Polanski, Singer, Spacey—who were previously given a pass indicates a shift in social consciousness, the current #MeToo movement is more complex, and more ambiguous, than it appears. Beyond the simple narrative of the triumph of righteousness over evil, #MeToo has the capacity to expose our society's collective trauma and complicity—which continue to perpetuate themselves today, in both mainstream and queer communities.

There was a decided lack of response to my attempts to find interviewees for this piece to speak to the experience of being abused and silenced by powerful queer people. Those who did express some interest insisted on giving their stories anonymously and in vague, almost inscrutable terms. They spoke about wanting to protect their abusers. They spoke about wanting to protect themselves.

As I write this essay in 2019, I am mindful of a handful of queer activists and artists and influencers who are famous within the niche of LGBTQ2 culture, who are also well known for certain patterns of behaviour. These patterns of behaviour lie somewhere on the spectrum between slightly creepy flirtation to ongoing sexual harassment. It is widely known who these individuals are. Yet no one says anything. They are not expendable to us yet, not the way some other members are—like, say, mentally ill trans women of colour sex workers.

We have been ignoring the abusive behaviour of queer celebrities for years, in some cases decades. When the protective ice around us melts—when our collective freeze response gives way to fight, to rage—who knows what will emerge?

Queer people live in what some psychologists call a "pathogenic environment" when it comes to speaking up versus remaining silent about abuse. A pathogenic environment is one that promotes illness, and in the context of psychology, mental illness. This alternative model sees illness as caused by the environment instead of the failure of the individual's body or mind.

Heteronormative society is pathogenic to queers and queer community because it hates us, it is violent to us, and it makes our stories invisible. Heteronormative society traumatizes us by demonizing our sexual expression—and so, we come to hate our sexual expression, our sexual identities, our sexual selves. We pass this hatred from one generation of queers to another in the form of unsafe and non-consensual sex practices, in slut-shaming and sex negativity and sexual aggression.

Society sexually traumatizes us, so we sexually traumatize one another.

Trapped in the fight-flight-freeze paradigm of sexual trauma, we become incapable of imagining solutions to sexual violence outside the realm of terror, death, and survival at any cost. We become incapable of imagining that our stories could be anything but destructive—and we create an understanding of justice in which this is true. Trauma dictates that justice must be punitive for us to feel safe. Paradoxically, of course, punitive justice tends to diminish our safety because it involves hurting other people and makes them far less likely to be accountable of their own volition. This paradigm in which every option leads to danger is the very definition of pathogenic—it is crazy-making; it is traumatizing.

In simple terms, this means that I cannot speak up about queers who have harmed me because that will result in them being harmed. It also means that if I do choose to speak up, they may try to avoid harm to themselves by suing, intimidating, or otherwise enacting more violence against me.

What would it take to create a community, a society, a world in which it was safe to tell our stories? Where we could melt the ice of our trauma without flooding the land with our grief? Popular answers to such questions tend to involve the words "restorative" or "transformative" justice, but the truth is that we have few models of what such justice might look like.

Queer writers adrienne maree brown, Leah Lakshmi Piepzna-Samarasinha, Ejeris Dixon, and Mia Mingus are among a handful of activists who have done groundbreaking work in this area. They advocate for a model of transformative justice that differentiates the concept of punishment from accountability and healing. In transformative justice the goal is not to mete out appropriate punishments but rather to transform the conditions that allowed harm to happen in the first place. Both victims and perpetrators of violence are understood to be integral parts of the community who require holding, healing, and support.

We need a whole movement of transformative justice thinkers and doers. Such a movement will require a fundamental shift away from trauma-based thinking toward courageousness and compassion. We will have to transform systems that centre *getting even* into systems that prioritize *getting better*.

Beyond the frameworks of justice that we apply to cases of sexual violence, I imagine that we will also have to develop new vocabularies for and ways of thinking about sexuality in general. We will have to let go of the idea that all forms of sexual boundary violations have the same intentions and impacts, and most especially, that sexual aggression is a special form of evil perpetrated only by monsters.

We will have to create a new form of sex positivity in which we understand that sex is sometimes wonderful, sometimes banal, sometimes uncomfortable, sometimes painful, sometimes violent—and sometimes a combination. We will have to find a way to distinguish between these different kinds of sexual experiences and the different kinds of behaviours that cause them so that we can properly address situations of harm. We will have to acknowledge that people can make mistakes about what their partners want, and that not all of these mistakes are intentional acts of evil—though we are still responsible when we make them.

Certainly, we will need to focus on preventing harm from happening rather than simply reacting, or not reacting, once harm has occurred. We need community practices and institutions that acknowledge the social conditions that breed violence—unchecked capitalism, misogyny, a policing system that profiles and fails to protect communities of colour, inadequate social services—and provide pathways to healing for hurt people. We need more hospitals and social programs, not more prisons and police.

And we will have to give up our defences, our time-worn defences of dissociation and numbness, as well as those of rage and revenge. We have to be able to care, even when it seems impossible because caring would destroy us. We have to believe that we will survive each other, that we will survive because of each other, because there is something waiting for us when the ice melts.

Queer community taught me that, once, a long time ago.

boundaries ii

your trauma is not mine
to hold. only you
can do that.
my pain is not yours
to heal.
only i
can do that.

I Hope We Choose Love
Notes on the Application of Justice

I'm not a big believer in justice. That skepticism extends to the notions of accountability, restorative justice, transformative justice, and most of the related terms that have taken hold in social justice culture—though I do very strongly believe in integrity, honesty, and personal honour. "Integrity" is a word you hear used fairly frequently in social justice circles, but honesty and honour, as I know them, are values that come to me through my Chinese family and upbringing. Honesty, in my family, means saying what you mean, even if it is unpopular. Honour means acting in a way that your ancestors would be proud of, even if it requires personal sacrifices to do so. However, "honour" is not a word you hear very much in social justice community, and I feel its distinct lack as an influence on activist conduct. I used to be much more of a believer in justice. I had drunk the Kool-Aid, though I wasn't ever really clear on exactly what justice meant. Rather ironically, I think a lot of people who are involved in social justice "activism"—scare quotes used because activism means a lot of different things to different people—aren't too clear on a working definition of justice. There is a subset of folks, of course, who have thought about the definition of justice a lot, but my sense is there is great disagreement and confusion among them. And why not? Justice is a pretty highfalutin philosophical concept. Over the years of my adolescence and early adulthood, I gave a great deal of myself to the idea of justice: time, energy, dignity, health. I made huge personal sacrifices to try to live up to the leftist ideals of justice, particularly accountability—which in the circles I ran in had a lot to do with using the right political language (which always changes) and doing all the right political things all the time, and then admitting in no uncertain terms that you were guilty and "problematic" when you were inevitably called out for infractions. There's actually a fair amount of good learning in that ideology—it teaches humility and listening to the voices of people in pain, which is pretty much always good in my book.

Unfortunately, the enactment of "justice" in radical leftism also played out in my life as a total invalidation of my boundaries (and I am not great at boundaries in the first place). For a time, I became quite valorized in my local community as a "good" upholder of social justice because I was very skilled at using the right language and doing the right things, and I tended to apologize unreservedly and perfectly when I "fucked up." I now recognize this as a skill born of trauma: the ability to ceaselessly and accurately scan the people in one's environment for a sense of what will please them, and then to enact it, no matter the cost to one's long-term health. This skill is a brilliant short-term survival strategy, as most trauma coping strategies are, designed to negotiate the unpredictability and cruelty of punishment—and unfortunately, a punishment narrative is deeply embedded in much of social justice.

I'm not a believer in justice because I have never gotten it from or against those who have harmed me. I really am not certain that it would be good for me if I did. I gave so much of myself trying to obtain justice for others, and it eventually rendered me traumatized and deeply disabled. I'm saying that as a literal statement of fact, not as a metaphor or to be melodramatic: I am now sick. I can't do things I used to be able to do without severe physical or psychological pain.

Many times in Social Justice Land, I was quite seriously taken advantage of and badly treated by white women in positions of power over me. This was done in public, when we were surrounded by so-called activists. Sometimes bystanders expressed sympathy to me in private afterward, but they never protected me or pushed back. I am, of course, angry about this, but I don't judge these vulnerable bystanders. I have done this exact same thing myself, many times: witnessed exploitation or violence, and then tried to be supportive without actually taking a stand. It has to do with fear—of punishment, of losing relationships and social status.

I have seen many white women call for justice in situations of personal conflict, violence, and abuse. I have seen others do it as well, but it tends to be white women who get the most attention, because white women are assumed to be inherently innocent. The ideological "innocence" I speak of here not only refers to the literal "not guilty of wrongdoing" but also encompasses a sense of "purity" or "virtue" that makes it blasphemous or deeply evil to be accused of harming a white woman. This, of course, is part of a historical legacy of the use of white womanhood as a justification for violence against people of colour—not too long ago, it was common for men of colour, especially Black men, to be lynched or imprisoned for supposedly endangering the virtue of white women, a practice that continues in more covert forms to this day.

Interestingly, I have also seen many people who are not white women attempt to claim the same kind of "innocence" in their own calls for justice—which entails, first, that the "innocent" person is seen as free of all and any responsibility for the situation and, second, that the "guilty" party is then rendered available for punishment. The logic then follows: if someone has done something bad, it is okay to be aggressive or even violent toward them.

We like punishment in Social Justice Land (lots of people, in many societies and subcultures, like punishment). Of course we do. It *feels good* to see someone who has hurt you receive a painful consequence for their actions, and we get that feeling by proxy when we see someone who has hurt someone else get punished. I don't think that's wrong in and of itself. I have lots of revenge fantasies, and they are very, very comforting to me at certain times. The problem is the enactment of punishment and revenge (and, no, I don't really see a meaningful distinction between punishment and revenge, though that is up for debate): pain and violence tend to replicate themselves, like a virus. Punishment does not end violence; on the contrary, it breeds it.

We like to think of our punishments as humane; that is, we like to think of them as not-punishment. We prefer to tell ourselves that our punishments are natural, justified consequences. Because punishment feels good in the moment, but it also makes us feel guilty. Leftists, in particular, do not like to see ourselves as perpetrators of cycles of violence because we claim to abhor violence. One notices, though, that the prison-industrial complex and legal criminal justice system also make claims to the moral sanctity of their use of punishments.

On the left, there is a nominal preference for "self-crit" and "accountability," rather than outright punishment, which usually means that the person who is understood to be guilty of an offence must immediately (immediately!) denounce themselves, often publicly, and then perhaps engage in some sort of reparative labour. This has the potential to be positively transformative but requires great skill to do successfully. We cannot be forced into immediate personal and spiritual growth—we must come to it willingly, or else we only end up disappointed at best and retraumatized at worst. This takes time, resources, and compassion on all sides. It takes compromise and is not immediately gratifying (or even gratifying in the medium term, frankly).

In social justice culture, accountability is enforced by public shaming and shunning, which often continues to affect the person's social standing long after the act of accountability/reparation is done. Collective measures for assessing the effectiveness of accountability processes and the degree of enforcement necessary are not in common usage; indeed, some people in social justice communities seem to prefer an endless bombardment of online call-outs to the resolution of conflict. The human dignity of someone who has done something "problematic" becomes deprioritized at best and outright trampled at worst.

We have all seen the dogpile of social media—people being relentlessly verbally attacked for making problematic statements despite their good intentions, or even for expressing legitimate differences of opinion. The movement seeks uniformity because uniformity and purity feel safe. This, too, is the language of trauma. I have also seen people doxed and stalked both online and in person. I have been stalked, by someone I had never met or spoken to, because they perceived me to be "abusing" them by not responding to a Facebook friend request. I have seen my friends spread rumours about others in community, advocating for shunning and ostracization over allowing ideological disagreements. On rare occasions, I have seen activists encourage the physical beating of abusive people in community.

As a whole, we have a tendency to escalate rather than de-escalate conflict. In our (rightful) desire to ensure that harm is not minimized or ignored, we use inflammatory language, binary concepts of right and wrong, and oversimplified narratives that more often than not increase tension and heighten rage and shame. We do not ask the questions that are central to transformative justice: *Why* has harm occurred? *Who* is responsible (beyond the individual perpetrator—as in, how is community implicated)? *How* can this harm be prevented in the future?

There are distinctions to made between punishment, justice, and healing. Punishment is a gratifying process of enacting revenge that also perpetuates cycles of violence. Justice is a slow process of naming and transforming violence into growth and repair; it is also frustrating and elusive—and rarely ends in good feelings. Healing is the process of restoration for those who have been hurt, and although justice can aid this process, my own experience is that healing is an individual journey that is almost entirely separate from those who have caused me harm. No apology, or amount of money or punishment, can give me back the person I was, the body and spirit I possessed, before I was violated. Only I can do that.

I do not have much faith in justice, but I have no choice but to believe in it. The other option is nihilism—total lack of faith in humanity—which I reject. We must reject nihilism because that way lies fascism. We must reject despair and embrace healing, slow and imperfect though it may be, and turn instead to love—love strong enough to live without faith. I am trying to embrace my own healing. I am trying to love my own painful, wounded life. As adrienne maree brown suggests, I am trying to embrace growth and constant transformation, like a flower growing in poisonous radiation. I am trying to let love emerge from my traumatized body.

So if we must do the work of justice, I suggest that we begin by redefining justice. Rather than a lens of punishment, consequence, or even accountability, we might try understanding justice through an ethic of love. Concrete steps toward building this love-based justice might look like the following:

- We must create flexible, working, practical definitions of justice so that we understand what we are doing and what values we share. There might need to be different definitions of justice for different contexts, but I believe that justice is the naming of harm and the transformation of the people *as well as the conditions* that perpetuated the harm.

- We must be open to the notion that survivors of harm can also be perpetrators of harm. Survival is not a badge of purity, nor a shield from accountability.

- We must invest deeply and fervently in the dignity of human life. We must not give in to the urge to do harm, even in justice's name. We must recognize, name, and transform the instinct to humiliate, harm, and coerce those we see as bad or as wrongdoers. No one is disposable.

- We must accept that we cannot force others to change their thinking or their beliefs. We can, however, set boundaries on violent behaviour, and we can enforce those boundaries.

- The practice of facilitating justice work demands complex skills and experience, and it requires great integrity. The facilitator of a justice process must operate honestly, transparently, and with an awareness of their own capacity for abusing the power of their role. As with any position of power, the facilitation of social justice may attract those more interested in that power than in the work itself, or it may present facilitators with the temptation to use that power unwisely. There must be guidelines and strategies to moderate the power of facilitators, and to prevent its misuse.

- Justice may not always be successful at making everyone, or anyone, feel good. We do not all have to like each other or be friends or share personal space. Justice should work toward reducing future harm through de-escalation, as well as ensuring that everyone has the basic resources they need to live, heal, and enjoy life—Yes! We have the right to enjoy our lives.

- Everyone has the right to access support while the work of justice is happening. Many seasoned practitioners of transformative justice suggest the use of "pods," or small groups of community to create agile networks of support.

- The community must accept its own responsibility for producing, condoning, and reproducing violence. We cannot spend years— decades—in community spaces watching people act badly and hurt each other, and making excuses for them, and then suddenly turn around and act shocked when an individual names that violence. We cannot pretend that we had no hand in covering up, minimizing, and even encouraging violence. We cannot have parties where everyone is deeply intoxicated, and physical, sexual, and verbal boundary-pushing is encouraged, and then act as though "abusers" are all sociopathic monsters who have infiltrated our otherwise perfect communities.

- We must love ourselves. We must encourage love—love that is radical, love that digs deep. Love that asks the hard questions, that is ready to listen to the whole story and keep loving anyway. Love for the survivors, love for the perpetrators, love for the survivors who have perpetrated and the perpetrators who have survived. Love for the community that has failed us all. We live in poison. The planet is dying. We can choose to consume each other, or we can choose love. Even in the midst of despair, there is always a choice. I hope we choose love.

the witch's manifesto
a freakish ethics for fearsome living in the monstrous world

preamble.

there is a creature who lives in the wood. there are many creatures who live in the wood. know thine enemy. know thine enemy. the village is at the edge of the wood. the fires burn bright in the village, the shadows are deep in the wood. in the wood where the creatures hide. the houses are in the village. the windows are open wide. on the edge of the wood, where the creatures hide. the people in the village are watching, are waiting, they have time to bide. in the village where the fires are bright. which do you choose? the village or the wood? where do you turn? where will you fly? to the fires that burn or the shadows that hide?

i. integrity
i would die
for my truth

i have already done this
several times

what would you do
for yours?

ii. honour
will you break bread?
will you break bone?
will you break promises?
will you break hearts?

i will break bread with all who are hungry
i will break the bones of those who would cage others
i will break promises at my peril
i will break hearts to free myself

iii. mercy
forgiveness is
the most powerful weapon
(and the most difficult to wield)
in the hands of a witch
it destroys the enemy
while healing yourself

iv. humility
i remember when humans were still trees. we wanted so much and hungered
so hard. they promised us heaven. we strained for the stars. we would have
swallowed them whole if we could. we forgot the language of the wind,
the grace of stillness. forgot sun songs and rain songs and kinship with
birds. we fell. we fall. we kneel, are kneeling. palms pressed to the ground,
praying: let it not be too late to return to our roots.

v. wisdom
never refuse
a gift from a witch
even when
it is wrapped in thorns

vi. strength
as
she
is
my
witness
i
shall
not
want
though
i
walk
in
the
valley
of
the
shadow
of
death
i
fear
no
evil
for
all
i
touch
i

change
and
all
i
touch
changes
me

vii. love
from within you
it devours

A School for Storytellers

I used to be enamoured with the idea of the poet, storyteller, or writer as a teacher, healer, and community facilitator—the belief that if you were going to put stories and ideas out into the world (or transmit stories from other people or generations), you had a responsibility to also engage in dialogue about those stories. I believed, and still do to some extent, that since your words touched real people and drew from real narratives, you had to be accountable for their impact in the world.

With time, however, I'm realizing just how much raw interpersonal intensity is directed toward storytellers—especially in the current moment of social media and celebrityism. Story-listeners are (as always) searching for personal meaning in the story, and it's only natural to assume that this meaning comes from the storyteller herself. This looks like questions for the storyteller, or anger directed at the storyteller, or a request for the storyteller to become a mentor, teacher, friend, replacement parent, or priest. Without always knowing it, audiences ask for non-consensual intimacy from the storyteller, partially because the act of receiving a story can feel incredibly intimate—a story can make us feel known and seen in ways that previously seemed impossible.

What is really important to understand, however, is that the storyteller is not the story. They are two separate things, even when the storyteller has created the story and is responsible for its existence. There's a difference between ethical storytelling—which is about sourcing story material ethically and building ethical relationships with one's audience—and assuming a role of caregiving and mentorship, which not every storyteller is willing or capable of doing. In the first place, a storyteller's job is partly to trouble meaning, to question meaning, to unseat our desire for moral certainty and universal truth. In the second, the storyteller is an artist, which is not in itself a qualification for healing work—it is a qualification for artistic work. And given that art frequently springs from a place of trauma, it is possible that artists are less suited on average than the general population for healing or mentoring work, which demands a certain level of stability from the healer or mentor.

Two things worry me: One is the tendency of the public to give power and credence to storytellers who fail to recognize their own limitations and then set themselves up as prophets, misusing their position to exploit or harm others. The other is the potential for harm to storytellers who are forced into positions of responsibility, scrutiny, and leadership that they may not be ready for. At extremes, storytellers are held hyper-accountable and are silenced, shamed, and/or stalked by story-listeners who are asking for too much.

Part of the problem is that there are not many schools for storytellers in this society where capitalism is everything, which for storytellers means that popularity and public image dictate the extent to which our art is considered valuable. Yes, there are schools that teach the technical aspects of storytelling (programs in creative writing, filmmaking, theatre), though some might argue that these schools are increasingly focused on teaching the marketing of stories rather than the making of stories. There are very few places where young creatives are nurtured and trained to take on the role and responsibilities of the storyteller, and to define this role for themselves. Where storytellers are supported to grapple with questions like: What *is* the role of a storyteller, in society and in community? What are the responsibilities and needs of a storyteller? Who is a storyteller accountable to? What should a storyteller *not* be expected to do? Why do we tell stories in the first place, and for whom?

The mythical school for storytellers of my dreams is a great wide garden by the sea. In this garden, there are huge rocks, chunks of lava hardened into stone and whittled by the wind into mysterious shapes that seem to be always changing. There is a pond full of golden fish with a wooden bridge arching over it that has a bench in the middle. There is a pavilion surrounded by wild rose bushes. And there are small wooden buildings, each with a fireplace and comfortable chairs and shelves full of books and puppets, costumes and masks and musical instruments.

Here, the student storytellers come to share and hone their gifts. They are tutored in the craft by mentors, each of whom has taken responsibility for the development of specific apprentices, selected for a careful match of interest, storytelling medium, and artistic style. Much time is spent in conversation, not only about the creation and refinement of stories (for it is believed and trusted that, given enough space and support, the stories will emerge from the bodies of the storytellers of their own accord) but also the development of a broad ethos of storytelling. Storytellers are prepared to answer the question—with answers that, surely enough, will change and evolve over time—of why they tell stories, and why people listen to them. They grapple with the purpose of story, the meaning of story, the who and what and where and when of telling a story. They practise the skills of creating and defending boundaries for themselves and the stories they bring into the world.

In this sacred temple of storytelling, there is room for expansiveness, for the release of trauma, but there is also a mindful awareness that the story and its telling are not and will never be everything. The story is a dream of healing, but it is not healing in and of itself. The spirit must heal itself. The story is a dream of the revolution, but it is not a revolution on its own. The people must make their own revolutions. The story is a dream of love and the seed of love and a map for love, but it takes people, not stories, to love each other. And here, the storyteller learns that the life of the story and the life of the teller are separate, though intertwined. The storyteller comes to understand that the telling of a good story is not the same as living a full life, though one informs the other. The storyteller learns that the love a story-listener has for the story is not the same as the love of one person for another. And so, the storyteller is at once freed to tell their stories and to live beyond and outside of them.

I can only dream of such a school for storytellers ...

how can i feel homesick?

how can i feel homesick
if i've never been home?

Part 3
LET US BELIEVE

How Neoliberalism Is Stealing Trans Liberation

In spring 2014, *Time* magazine put the ever-regal Laverne Cox on its cover and declared that the world had reached a "transgender tipping point." I have always loved that photograph. Staring out at us in her blue dress and heels, head raised high, Cox appears to be challenging the world: *Are you ready for us?* her eyes seem to ask. *Are you ready to celebrate us—and all the gifts we have to give?*

Trans, gender-nonconforming, and non-binary people have always had a great deal to offer the rest of humanity: historically, gender-nonconforming, third gender, and Two-Spirit individuals have been recognized as artistically and spiritually gifted in many societies across the globe. Although the ravages of European colonization have worked to suppress this cultural knowledge in many communities, it remains alive and relevant today. The resilience and brilliance of trans people have a long and proud lineage, rooted in the ancestral memory of colonized peoples worldwide.

Politically, trans people, particularly trans feminine people of colour, have paved the way for LGBT rights. As the legend goes, a trans woman (or "transvestite," which was once a more socially accepted term among trans feminine individuals) of colour threw the first brick during the Stonewall riots widely considered to have sparked the modern gay liberation movement.

Perhaps more importantly, however, it was the work of trans feminine activists such as Marsha P. Johnson and Sylvia Rivera—who called themselves variously gay, drag queens, transvestites, and transgender—that pushed the boundaries of the queer liberation movement to include youth of colour, queer sex workers, homeless youth, and other extremely marginalized groups. The legacy of those activists' work finds its home today in the work of contemporary trans and genderqueer community groups such as the Audre Lorde Project, the Sylvia Rivera Law Project, and many others.

Trans liberation politics, forged in the fires of oppression and the struggle to survive were and are the revolutionary spark of queer resistance.

Five years after the so-called "transgender tipping point," however, not much seems to have changed for the majority of trans people in 2019. There is a strange disconnect between the social transformation that appears to have taken place in the media and the ongoing reality of violence, deprivation, and discrimination that trans people continue to experience.

There are more trans people on television than ever before, but trans youth remain vastly disproportionately homeless and suicidal. Trans people's visibility has skyrocketed, but anti-trans legislation and discrimination remain rampant. Trans rights are debated more and more frequently in major news outlets, but trans women who are Black, brown, and sex workers continue to be assaulted and murdered regularly.

How can this be happening? How can we be living in a world where trans identities are discussed seemingly endlessly, but trans people are no safer for it? Where the existence of trans celebrities—even trans millionaires—is possible, but trans people as a class remain seriously oppressed on every legal and social level?

Our revolutionary fire burns bright as always, but I am afraid that it is being misdirected, co-opted. Something is stealing trans liberation, and we must understand what that is—and resist it.

When I was a social worker, I spent a lot of time supporting trans youth and gender-nonconforming children (who are too young to identify with the word "trans"), as well as their parents. I often saw parents who were extremely reluctant to help their trans kids pursue social and medical transition. Interestingly, I also met a significant number of parents who were very eager to pursue hormone therapy for their kids, as well as to change the gender markers on their children's legal documents. The hope, many of the latter type of parents told me, was that "no one needs to know" that their child was trans.

As I see it, the positions of both types of parents come from feelings of love, and protectiveness—the most natural thing in the world for a parent to feel. This protective instinct is, I believe, inherent to parents and guardians of children across cultures. What parent doesn't want their kid to live a "normal" life, with all the privileges that come with "normalcy"?

Yet "normalcy" in this era of advanced capitalism, class warfare, and political instability is a loaded concept that comes with an oft-forgotten history of oppression. Here in the colonized West, the standard for a "normal" life is not only cisgender but also white, middle class, monogamous, abled, and (perhaps except for a certain form of upper-class white homonormativity that is beginning to be promoted in contemporary liberal society) heterosexual.

Although it has become more and more common for progressive mainstream media outlets to feature stories of trans kids who transition young, I find it very interesting that the majority of these children are white, blond, middle class—and very, very passable as cisgender.

As a visibly racialized trans woman who often does not pass for cis, I sometimes found it strange to provide support to white, middle-class parents who anxiously asked me well-intentioned questions such as: *Will my trans child still be able to marry? Have children? Will they still be able to travel? Will they pass? Will they experience any discrimination in school, employment, housing, dating?*

Sometimes, it felt like the implication was: *Will my child end up like you? Unpassable, visibly marginalized? Or, worse, will they end up like "those trans people" who do survival sex work and are murdered in the dark?*

Transition is a fundamental right that all trans people, of all ages, should have access to. But I believe that transition, ideally, should be offered to us as one option of many for bodily autonomy and self-expression. It should not be something that we have to do to make ourselves more acceptable to others, or to hide our transness from the world.

And transition should most certainly not be a privilege where the best options for hormone replacement therapy, surgery, and fertility treatments are reserved only for those who can afford them.

These parents expressed a certain desire that I think is mirrored in many—if not all—marginalized people. I feel it in myself. It is the desire to live the life of the privileged class, to exist without being marked as different, to fit inside the system the way white, middle-class people do.

When parents came to me with those anxious questions, I forced myself to take a breath. I remembered my responsibilities as a therapist, a healer. I thought of my own commitment to helping trans kids achieve an easier life than mine. I gave some answers, and I asked some questions of my own:

Yes, your child will still be able to travel and find a partner and probably get married, if that's what they want. They might be able have a child biologically, depending on what they decide to do with their body, and they also might be able to adopt.

They might experience some discrimination in different parts of their lives. How do you think you can support them in getting through it? Have you experienced discrimination in your own life, and how did you get through that?

Is it more important to you for your child to have an easy, "normal" life or a fulfilling, liberated one?

The social system in which we live is the result of advanced, decaying capitalism and colonization: it is neoliberalism. Neoliberalism is, I believe, the force that is banking the fire of trans liberation.

"Neoliberalism," a term coined in the 1970s, refers to the dominance of free market capitalism in every aspect of public and private life. Under neoliberalism, it is assumed that people are not entitled to any rights, goods, or services—including privacy, health care, housing, and education—that they can't afford to buy. Under neoliberalism, traditionally government-run institutions such as hospitals, schools, and prisons are corporatized and run for profit.

Increasingly, this economic model is overtaking almost every country in the world.

Neoliberalism erodes human rights movements in an insidious way. It co-opts the thinking and operations of human rights activism by creating fear and scarcity so that our political goals are forced to focus not on envisioning a better future for all but on personal survival. Hoarding resources, assimilation into the status quo, and no-holds-barred individualism are second nature in neoliberal thinking.

We have already seen how neoliberalism has, largely, co-opted the mainstream queer rights movements of the sixties and seventies. LGBT rights once constituted a radical political movement based around concepts of free love, socialism, and solidarity with other marginalized groups. In later decades, however, it became increasingly focused on the narrower goals that primarily served the interests of white, middle-class, cisgender gays and lesbians: the rights to marry, adopt children, serve in the military, and work in prestige professions.

Meanwhile, the anti-poverty, anti-homelessness, and pro–sex work activism of trans feminine activists of colour such as Sylvia Rivera and Marsha P. Johnson's Street Transvestite Action Revolutionaries (STAR) group was pushed to the background. Seeking respectability, mainstream gay advocacy groups publicly distanced themselves from trans causes and leaders.

So although we have seen certain gay rights "victories," such as the right to marry in many countries and the repeal of the "Don't ask, don't tell" US military policy, the neoliberal status quo itself remains largely unchallenged. The rich remain rich and the poor remain poor, and a relatively tiny group of queer folks got to join the rich while most of us stayed behind.

Nowadays, as the "transgender tipping point" picks up steam, I am watching the rise of a new generation of trans rights activists, and I wonder which direction they are going to choose: Neoliberal assimilation? Or revolution?

When I was a social worker, I started to see more and more usually white, middle-class youth and children coming out as trans. It's beautiful. They are brave and resilient, and sometimes, their families actually support their transition and advocate for their access to health care and education.

Yet I see just as many trans youth, mostly of colour, who are estranged from their families, living in shelters or on the street, blocked from accessing the resources they need for day-to-day survival, let alone medical transition and higher education.

Trans visibility is greater than ever; trans rights awareness is at an all-time high. Yet the class divide between trans people grows and grows.

In 2015, a year after *Time*'s "tipping point" cover article, the world watched multi-millionaire reality television star and former Olympic athlete Caitlyn Jenner win both a *Glamour* Woman of the Year Transgender Champion Award and an ESPY Arthur Ashe Courage Award. That same year, Jenner stated in an interview that "the hardest thing about being a woman is figuring out what to wear," betraying a profound disconnection from the real daily lives of the majority of cis and trans women alike.

The lionization of Caitlyn Jenner by the mainstream media establishment has already been roundly critiqued by queer and feminist writers. However, what I find politically significant about Jenner is not her personal merit, or lack thereof, but rather the growing phenomenon of transgender celebrityism and its connection to the neoliberal myth that things are improving for trans people as a class, whereas in many ways it appears the opposite is true.

The myth of exceptionalism has always been a cornerstone of neoliberal philosophy—the idea that since a few people can "make it" under capitalism, then everyone else can too. It is a myth that conflates the success of an individual with the prosperity of their entire class, and it is used to hide the barriers of systemic discrimination and violence.

Neoliberal thinking says, if a Black man has become president of the United States, racism in America must be over. Black folks who complain about police brutality and discrimination must just not be trying hard enough to succeed. If Caitlyn Jenner can get facial feminization surgery and win awards, if Jazz Jennings can have her own reality show, and if Andreja Pejić can model in *Vogue*, then trans people everywhere must not have it that bad. All the rest of us need to do is get famous too.

The truth is the capacity for trans celebrities to shift the realities of trans people as a class under neoliberalism is very limited—even when those celebrities are actively involved in efforts to resist.

Laverne Cox and Janet Mock, for example, are two famous Black trans women who have taken pains to stay connected to grassroots trans and racial activism. Yet they remain constrained by the nature of American celebrity culture, which is inherently elitist and exclusive. In order to remain celebrities, they must tread carefully between glamour and grassroots, between speaking truth to power and toeing the line.

Representation of trans identities in fashion, television, and film is important. We need to see ourselves reflected in the stories around us. But we must be critical of whose stories are told, and why. We must remember that representation and revolution are not at all the same thing.

Put another way: Why did Caitlyn Jenner, a wealthy Republican reality television star, win an award for inspiring trans people to be courageous, whereas CeCe McDonald, a Black trans woman who was imprisoned for physically defending herself from a transphobic attack on her life, did not?

I am not the first trans person to make these arguments. As a diasporic trans woman of colour, I come from a history of brilliant thinkers and fierce activists.

And I will be far from the last. As a generation of young trans people like myself, with access to education and a public platform, emerges, we will each have to ask ourselves the question: What battles will we choose to fight, and for whom? Will those of us with the greatest chance of succeeding within the systems of the neoliberal status quo fight for our piece of the pie alone, or will we try to overturn the tables of capitalism and white supremacy, as our revolutionary foreparents did before us?

I know that I don't want to live in a world where trans people can only access medical transition care if they have the insurance to pay for it. I want everyone to get the health care they need.

I don't want to live in a world where middle-class trans people can use public washrooms that match their gender identities, but homeless trans people are barred from public spaces. I want to live in a world where everyone has a home.

I don't want to live in a world where trans people can join the military or law enforcement and participate in the violent oppression of people of colour around the world. I want to live in a world without wars or police brutality.

I don't want to live in a world where trans people are put in prisons that match their gender identity. I want to live in a world without prisons.

I don't want to live in a world where a handful of trans celebrities make millions of dollars while the rest of us struggle to survive. I want to live in a world where we all have what we need to thrive.

I don't want to live in a world where some trans people are considered normal and others are considered freaks. I want to live in a world where all of our freakish, ugly, gorgeous magnificence is celebrated for its honesty, glory, and possibility.

My dear trans kindred—weird sisters, brothers grim and gay, siblings-in-arms: What kind of a world do you want to live in?

siblings

how could you do this to me? said the Sun to the Moon
how could you steal my light?
a tear rolled down her pale cheek.
i just wanted to be seen, said the Moon.

The Ties That Bind, the Family You Find, Or: Why I Hate Babies

There isn't a queer in the world who doesn't pine for the perfect family. It stands to reason, since the vast majority of us have complicated—to say the least—relationships with our parents. Even those of us lucky enough to be born into accepting families still feel that longing, like a compass in the heart, always pointing toward a distant place where we are safe at last, where there are no shameful secrets, where we are held and nourished and protected as perfectly as a baby bird still in its shell.

This is why the concept of chosen family is woven so deeply into the fabric of queer community culture: where the bonds of blood have failed us time and again, we hope that our friends, lovers, and mentors will fill the void.

We dream of relationships that stand against the test of time and gay drama, for better or worse, in sickness and in health. Shut out of the heteronormative institutions of marriage and the nuclear family for most of history, queers have traditionally turned to more daring and creative notions of kinship and sharing the future.

When I was first entering queer community in the urban centres of Vancouver and Montreal, I often heard other young people talking about their radical plans for growing up together.

Some of us longed for monogamy and middle-class domesticity—for a gay version of the kind of existence our parents had taught us was worth wanting. But it was more popular, especially among the university queers with asymmetrical haircuts and a penchant for citing Michel Foucault in everyday conversation, to lean toward polyamory and collective living.

Gay marriage, the university queers said (often with more than a hint of superiority), was bourgeois and passé. So was the nuclear family and homeownership. The racist, sexist, colonial heteropatriarchy would never be undone by the assimilation of queer love into neoliberal modes of family. We weren't going to be co-opted!

We were going to build queer urban housing collectives, gay land shares in partnership with Indigenous nations, trans-inclusive lesbian nature communes run by consensus. We would take in scores of LGBTQ teenagers kicked out of the house by their parents and teach them the ways of the Radical Queer. We would learn how to grow crops and make our own vegan cheese. We would raise chickens and cows and free-range unicorns and go riding across the fields, our multicoloured hair flowing in the wind.

Don't scold me too harshly for my sarcasm, dear reader. I need to poke fun at the revolutionary overenthusiasm of university queers because I was one of them. I disavowed capitalist individualism, decried assimilationist gay politics, denounced the nuclear family. I wanted to escape the trap that my parents seemed to have fallen into, of endless striving for material success and consequent perpetual dissatisfaction. I wanted to live differently, vibrantly, with my friends in an endless circle of share and share alike.

We looked to the legends of movements past and present for inspiration: Sylvia Rivera and Marsha P. Johnson, founders of the STAR house for trans sex workers in New York City. The gay faerie sanctuaries of the 1970s, and the faerie enclaves that still exist, scattered across the world. The radical care work that occurred between lesbians and gays of the ACT UP movement and the AIDS crisis.

The lineage of radical queer kinship runs deeper than blood. Why would we ever need marriage and babies and condominiums when we had the Revolution and each other?

The problem was, reader, that the Revolution never arrived (or, at least, it hasn't yet). The babies, however, did come for us.

I have a running private joke that's just between me and myself (and now you, dear reader) that I hate babies—"queerspawn," or the children of queer couples, most of all. It's not a very funny joke, really, unless you take it in the lighthearted yet bittersweet spirit in which it is meant. Allow me to explain myself:

I don't really *hate* babies. As a general rule, actually, I like them very much. They're quite cute, and they have good skin, and when they're clean, they smell like fresh bread. Any of my child-rearing friends will tell you that I am rather good with babies, for someone who doesn't have any of my own. I know how to hold them and change their diapers, and I am an excellent sport when they spit up on my good clothing.

So, no, my problem isn't with babies in and of themselves. My problem is that babies seem to be stealing all of my friends and, with them, my hopes for the future.

I suppose I ought to backtrack. In between entering community in our late teens/early twenties and growing into our late twenties and early thirties, the radical queers of my generation underwent, or so it appeared to me, a fundamental political and relational shift. We became more jaded, less idealistic. Our chosen families began to fragment, torn asunder by romantic breakups, political falling-outs, and in some cases, intimate partner violence and sexual assault.

The community began to feel less like an actual community and more like a scene comprised of various cliques loosely bound together by aesthetics and fuzzily defined politics.

When queers reverently tell the story of Marsha P. Johnson, Sylvia Rivera, and the STAR House, they don't often talk about how Marsha P. and Sylvia dealt with political infighting or breakups among the STAR residents.

The older my queer cohort and I get, the further away our dream of creating a life with our chosen families seems to slide. The white punk trust fund kids—ironically, the most vocal in their denunciation of gay assimilation back in our teenage days—were the first to go: one by one, they cast off their anarcho-punk ripped denim and slunk off to law school. Then, many of us who were raised by racialized and working-class parents to always have a backup plan started to pursue whatever options for economic stability were available: non-profit jobs, art and academic grants, commercial sex work.

Of course, not all of us had access to the same opportunities, and that is still the case. Some queers are more upwardly mobile than others. Some queers have no choice but to live collectively, hand to mouth, sharing whatever space and resources are available.

But even across the various economic classes the queer community of my adolescence has broken into, I am noticing the tide turning. We still want kinship, and intimacy. We still want a future. But, all around me, I see queer acquaintances and friends settling into monogamy (or something like it) and nuclear units (more or less). That is to say, more and more of us are settling down, getting married, and having babies (give or take the marriage part).

I probably should have seen it coming. I know that it isn't a bad thing, strictly speaking, or even at all. People marched and fought and died, after all, so that we could get married and raise children. I know this.

I know this.

Between 2017 and 2019, nine babies were born into the network of friends and acquaintances that I call my queer community. And more are on the way. Every day, I talk to at least one person about their plans to give birth to and raise a child. Their eyes are always so full of life. So full of hope, and fervour.

I used to see my friends' eyes shine that way when we talked about living together, starting a collective, learning how to cultivate food from the land. Growing old together. Dying together.

A new life coming into the world is a joyful thing, and we rightfully celebrate that. Especially for queers, whose bodies and right to reproduction are always called into question, childbirth and child-rearing take on an especially deep significance.

So when my friends burst into the room, eyes shining, overflowing with both excitement and anxiety to tell me the news about their forthcoming babies, I celebrate with them—I truly do. I want to be there; I want to do right by them.

But there is also a certain heaviness that settles in the chambers of my heart of hearts, a slow acceptance of what it means when your dear friend, your chosen family member, to whom you are neither a spouse nor co-parent, is having a child: Your place in their life has changed. The meaning of your bond is different, perhaps not lessened but deprioritized, certainly. I know this: I was a family therapist, for God's sake.

Babies, the having and raising of them, irrevocably alter the ways in which new parents interact with and perceive the world around them, the community, and the future. To be a good parent means that the well-being of the child comes first—before friendship, before political projects, before anything else. And in the capitalist society we live in, which largely separates child-raising from community by emphasizing the nuclear family as the building block of society, this means that parents are set apart from non-parents, often irrevocably. In our society, parents are meant to put their children before anyone else, and non-parents are given no role in the raising of children outside of heavily boundaried professions like teaching and social work.

Before gay marriage was legalized in Canada and many parts of the United States, it was common for queer activists to offhandedly refer to heterosexuals as "breeders." This isn't to say that queers didn't have children before the advent of gay marriage—queers have had and raised children throughout history, though often covertly—rather, it signified a markedly different relationship to family and generationality.

Because queers had limited access to the benefits of the nuclear family—such as inheritance, parental rights, and care work—and because the line between friends and lovers is so often blurred in queer community, friendship took on a kind of deep and lasting primacy for queers that does not exist in heteronormative society. Generational knowledge is passed not from parent to child but through an informal system of mentorship.

When queers are sick and dying, it is our friends, not our family, whom we most often rely on to care for us. When we are suicidal, our friends talk us down. When we are broke, our friends lend us money. When we are beaten up by homophobes and transphobes, evicted by our landlords, kicked out by our parents, thrown out or assaulted by our partners, our friends take us in.

For so much of my life, I have lived by this unwritten law: *Queers take care of queers. No one else will.*

What does it mean, then, that so many of my queer cohort are pairing off and having children? On the one hand, it means that queer rights have come very far indeed, at least for some. On the other, it means that our understanding of queer kinship must necessarily change, probably for better and for worse at once.

What does it mean to be part of a *chosen* family when it must abide with *biological* and *legal* family? That is to say, if my chosen queer sibling gets married and has a baby, where do I fit in? Is *chosen* family another way of saying *second-best* family?

I've taken a turn toward the cynical in the past few years. Once, I would have said I would die for the ideals of chosen family and a revolutionary society. Now, having literally risked my health and safety a time or two for those ideals, I have become much more concerned with my individual, material well-being:

I live alone. I refuse to do activism unless it directly serves my own purposes. I prioritize time alone, economic sustainability, a very small number of friends, and my romantic partnership (not always in that order). My parents would be proud—or at least, they'd say, "We told you so."

Who is going to share my life with me? Who is going to fight with me, take care of me, grow old and die with me? Who will I take care of? Who would I die for? I think about these questions all the time these days. I still have a chosen family, but I think queers are confused about what we mean by the word "family," unsure of where we are going and what we hope to become.

Perhaps I am being immature to begrudge my friends their babies. I wonder if every young adult, queer or otherwise, goes through this period of transition, of wondering where they belong as they watch new biological families spark to life all around them. I wonder if I am supposed to grow past this, give up my fantasy of collective living and free-range unicorn husbandry, and get serious about finding a boyfriend, a husband, with whom to settle down.

The truth is I have thought about having children of my own. A more revolutionary trans woman—the kind I think I am supposed to be—would dream about living in polyamorous configurations, agrarian communes, collectives where children are raised by intergenerational pods of kindred spirits. Yet in my heart of hearts, I dream of raising babies with a sweet and hapless heterosexual man in a suburban home with shiny stainless steel appliances and a front lawn. We would spend sleepless nights tending to our colicky baby, fret over grades and school lunches, argue about whether to force the kid to take piano lessons (I would be a firm yes on that). We would worry ourselves sick over our child's first sleepover, first drunken party, first car accident. We would try not to hover too much as they grew up and away from us. We would make each other promise not to die first.

But I am a post-transition trans woman. I cannot have babies, not in the biological sense. Adoption is theoretically possible but in reality a giant challenge, given that child welfare agencies tend to systemically discriminate against trans people and regard trans women in particular with suspicion.

As for finding that lifelong partner with whom to grow old and die— well, all trans women know that romantic love is like hope: at best, a fickle creature; at worst, a dangerous beast.

There is a scene at the end (spoiler alert) of the classic children's novel *Peter Pan* when the eponymous hero comes to find his beloved Wendy in London—only to discover that in the time he has been away in Neverland, Wendy has grown up, gotten married, and had a daughter. A compulsive caregiver to my friends, I have always thought of myself as Wendy among the Lost Boys of queer community, but now I am beginning to understand how Peter must have felt.

Sooner or later, we all must leave Neverland. But where do we go next?

What does it mean to grow up? To face the future? What do queers owe each other, and what do we owe ourselves? These are the questions that our queer generation is facing, as did the ones before us. Although some might say that growing up means assimilating into heteronormative society, this is not really an option for many queers. It is not an option for me.

The world is collapsing all around us, geopolitically speaking. Climate change and the resurgence of fascism in the Global North are the tip of the proverbial iceberg. We are living in the beginning of the end, in the apocalypse. We are living in a time of flame, and the old dreams are dying: Capitalism. Communism. Individualism. Collectivism.

We must choose to place our hope in the magic and resilience of queers, in our capacity to break apart and reform, to invent possibility from ash. I choose to believe that we can do it, that there will be a place for me somewhere in the swirling chaos we call the future. I choose to believe that we can mourn what we used to be and love what we are and honour what comes next.

We can live and celebrate life. Together.

there's another girl out there

somewhere in the vast expanse of the multiverse. trans. chinese. born in the west with a heart full of eastern winds and fox's fire. she took a different turn than you did, though, somewhere back where the roads wind tight around the spool of all our silly, mundane, ultimately-irrelevant-in-the-grand-scheme-of-things fates.

she chose money. you chose art. she chose safety. you chose adventure. she, filial piety. you, self-actualization. she, self-preservation. you, self-sacrifice. she, common sense. and you, revolution.

she works in a bank somewhere, probably, or maybe a mid-level marketing company. she has her own cubicle by the window on the 16th floor, she decorates it with posters made from the covers of old pulp science-fiction and fantasy novels. her job is nothing; the decently paid absence of vocation filled by spreadsheets and memos and emails, days full of language and little meaning. her co-workers are patronizing—they like nothing more than welcoming her to womanhood, a state she's existed in more or less comfortably for ten years—but kind. she likes to work late, not out of any sense of loyalty to the company, but because she enjoys silence and watching the sun set. on evenings when it rains or snows, she pretends she is living inside a giant snow globe. she takes the train home to her boyfriend, a white boy who drinks a little too much with his buddies on the weekend but is sweet and decent overall. they watch movies together, cuddle, have boring but affectionate sex.

they won't have children. he doesn't want them, and she can't. that, at least, you still have in common.

there are things she wants and fears, this commonsensical girl who visits her parents every other weekend and endures their misplaced advice with politely concealed boredom, but she doesn't think about them much. she has nice clothes, a pretty condominium she is ever so slowly paying the mortgage on. on weekends she goes jogging, cooks meals, goes to coffee with friends. she used to volunteer at the local queer community centre, but she doesn't do that anymore. the politicking and infighting are endless there, a serpent eating its own tail, and she's smart enough to know that this isn't something she needs or wants. *don't let drowning people pull you underwater.* she learned that in lifeguarding classes at the community centre when she was a teenager, and unlike you, she took the advice to heart.

it's not so bad, being trans and middle class and chinese, at least not in this big city where difference is common, if not always celebrated—is it? the catcalls and stares, bureaucratic inconveniences and social gaffes, she just ignores. she's a skilled survivor, and she knows to appreciate what she's got. she tries not to lust after what she doesn't have, though the wind blows the heart in her hard sometimes, tugging at her ribs, making her chest ache.

on summer nights, she likes to leave her boyfriend sleeping in bed and ride the elevator all the way up to the rooftop garden of the condo building. there's a pool there, with water salty as tears and blue as freedom. she dives in, holds her breath as long as she can. thinks about mermaids. whales. jellyfish. buried treasure. she holds and holds and holds her breath, 'til she can hear her heart pounding, lungs screaming. her vision blurs and her head spins. she comes back up, breaks the surface. she floats on her back, looking at the stars.

somewhere, she thinks, *out in the vast multiverse, there is another girl.*

Rediscovering Identity at My Grandfather's Funeral
An Ethnic Trans Story

When the first Chinese migrant workers came to Canada in the 1800s, they believed that the bones of any man who died in this cold, cruel land had to be sent home to be buried in his ancestral village. Otherwise, his spirit would become a "hungry ghost," a lost soul doomed to wander this barren place for eternity. There were many unfortunate souls—workers whose broken bodies were lost in the landslides created by dynamite used to build the Canadian Pacific Railway, poor people whose families could not afford the passage back to China—who suffered this fate. They still walk among us, the old-timers say.

Today, in the twenty-first century, I can't help but think that maybe it's me and my fellow second-, third-, and fourth-generation Chinese Canadian queers who are the hungry ghosts. We are destined to live in the space between homelands: Too queer for Chinatown. Too "whitewashed" for the urban queer scenes of Mainland China, Hong Kong, Taiwan—places where most of us have never lived anyway. Too Asian for the Village, which loves its pretty white boys so much.

My *yeh yeh*, paternal grandfather, died eight years ago, in 2011. I never told him I was trans, which I'm not certain he would have understood anyway. I don't know if there's a word for "trans" in *toisanhua*, my family's ancestral tongue. Contemporary Cantonese and Mandarin have developed a variety of roughly equivalent terms, but my *yeh yeh* was a working-class man who grew up in rural China during the civil war and the Japanese invasion and never attended high school. I assume he wouldn't have learned those words. I guess I assume a lot of things about *Yeh Yeh*.

I never really learned to speak any dialect of Chinese very well. I knew *Yeh Yeh* from the time I was born, but our conversations were limited to a handful of broken sentences here and there in three different languages—English, Cantonese, *toisanhua*. Three generations of stories slipped through the cracks in the words between us, two whole lifetimes lost in translation.

Still, some things stay sacred, no matter how far from home you go. In Chinese tradition, when an elder passes away, the eldest son of each child of the departed bears the coffin at the funeral. For my family, that was me. It didn't matter that I was now a girl. I was also, still, the eldest son. I had a duty to fulfill, a role to play, an obligation of blood. This is Chinese love, the truest love.

I want to take a moment here to note that white people are always asking queers of colour to tell them the "ethnic gay story." "Was it hard to come out to your family?" they ask eagerly, eyes bright with hunger. "Are they very traditional?" (which is to say, queerphobic). (It is taken for granted that the traditions of non-white cultures are queerphobic.) Liberal white people love the ethnic gay story. It confirms their belief in the superiority of whiteness and assuages their sublimated guilt over the queerphobia and racism that are still rooted deep within white-dominant, colonial Western society.

What the ethnic gay story misses is that the queer children of diaspora are not the passive victims of our villainous, ignorant families—or at least, not in the way that white people like to imagine. Our relationships with our blood, ourselves, are more complicated than that.

So I don't believe that when I flew to Victoria for the funeral, leaving my punk queer femme clothes behind, that I was being forced to leave my womanhood behind as well. As I washed off my makeup and dressed in a black suit and tie, for all the world my parents' son again, I was not choosing between being trans and being Chinese. What I chose was the strength of my family's values—loyalty, lineage, the fulfilment of duty, gratitude to one's elders—*and* the magic of queerness: transformation, change, adaptation, and resiliency.

So perhaps it isn't as strange as it seems that when I took the weight of the rosewood coffin that held my *yeh yeh*'s body in my gloved hands, lifting it up with five of my male cousins, I felt stronger and more certain in who I was than I ever had before. In that moment, on that island an ocean so far away from where my ancestors were born, I knew who I was: My mother's daughter. My father's son. A woman as Chinese as they come, as strong as the iron and the bones my ancestors laid in the ground to build the spine of this colonized nation, as queer as a new moon rising.

It's hard to walk with ghosts on your shoulders, but when you learn to listen to what they're saying, you realize that they're telling the story of who you are.

A traditional Chinese funeral ends with a rite of cleansing. A fire is lit in front of the doorway of the departed's home, and the family in mourning jumps over the flames before re-entering the house. The flames purify the living of bad luck, and the rising smoke lifts what remains of the departed one's spirit up into heaven. This is an old, old custom—older than the arrival of Christianity in Asia, older than the spread of Buddhism into China, older than Taoism.

My family approximated this ritual by lighting some rolls of newspaper on fire in my *yeh yeh*'s driveway. Picture it: forty Chinese people, spanning four generations, dressed in funeral wear, standing around a pile of burning paper in a driveway in the middle of suburban Victoria.

As I prepared to leap over the fire, I bowed my head and closed my eyes. I thought about *Yeh Yeh*, the things I would never say to him, the things he would never know about me. In the distance, I could hear the sound of sirens.

And then the sounds weren't so distant.

Racing down the street, sirens blaring and lights ablaze, came a small fleet of fire trucks and police cars. They squealed up to my *yeh yeh*'s house and several uniformed officers jumped out. The elders of the family recoiled, scandalized; the little kids darted behind their parents; and those of us in our twenties and thirties stepped forward protectively.

As it turned out, the neighbours had been watching through their windows, and someone had called 911. Lord knows what they must have said. *An Asian cult in formal wear is performing a Satanic ritual in someone's front yard.* My grandparents had lived in that suburb with their white neighbours for more than twenty years, only to have my *yeh yeh*'s last rites desecrated by racism. Some things never change.

I like to think my *yeh yeh* would have laughed to hear what had happened at his funeral. I like to think he'd acknowledge what I did for him with quiet approval. I like to think that someday I'll tell him the story in the place where the ancestors live, a place between the worlds, where every story can be told and understood.

trauma said

trauma said,
"you cannot leave me,"
said, "i live in your bones."
 trauma said, "only i have never left you. i
am all that you know."
i said to trauma,
"i am so much more than you."

The Chinese Transsexual's Guide to *Cheongsam*

This is the story of my womanhood, told through the outline of a dress. Sooner or later in every Chinese girl's life, there comes a reckoning with the *cheongsam*. Even if you don't know the word, you still know what I'm talking about: that dress with the high collar, body-hugging silhouette, and slits up the outside of both thighs.

The dress so often associated with the stereotype of East Asian women as at once uptight and demure yet nymphomaniacally hypersexual; in other words, the misogynist's perfect fantasy doll. The dress that has been linked for the past 100 years with Chinese (and, arguably, East Asian in general) women's femininity and sexuality, and that still appears everywhere, haunting Chinese women, from runways to thrift shops to drag stages to pornos.

Also known in Mandarin as the *qipao* and to the uninitiated simply as the "Chinese dress," the name of the *cheongsam* comes from Cantonese, meaning "long garment." Once a loose-fitting unisex national outfit introduced by the Manchurian conquerors in the 1600s, the *cheongsam* took a decided turn for the modern and sexy in 1920s Shanghai, where the influence of colonial Europe held sway over fashion and cultural production. In 1960, actress Nancy Kwan burst onto the silver screen in the now cringe-inducingly Orientalist film *The World of Suzie Wong*, sweeping Hollywood with her portrayal of a sexpot Chinese escort who seduces a white American man, all the while dressed in slinky, revealing *cheongsam*.

So the *cheongsam* has become inextricably linked with Chinese femininity in the mainstream cultural imagination. And like Chinese women ourselves, the *cheongsam* has acquired a strange double connotation, seen as both conservatively traditional and intensely erotic. Caught between those extremes, the texture of our humanity, our womanhood, is lost in translation.

Perhaps this is why in Hong Kong, Taiwan, Mainland China, Singapore, Canada, and the US—and everywhere else that Chinese people live—it is rare for Chinese women to wear *cheongsam*—which was once a ubiquitous staple of middle-class daywear—except for cultural holidays and weddings. Meanwhile, cheap, bastardized versions of the dress are popular as Halloween and sexy dress-up costumes among hipster white women.

Lately, I've found myself obsessed with *cheongsam*. I've scoured Toronto's thrift stores and the internet for them. I've worn them to work and out on the town. I've spent an irrational amount of money on them. Unlike the gaudy silk red-and-gold versions of cultural stereotype, there are versions made for office and evening wear, in a wide range of fabrics and patterns, from paisley to polka dots.

As a trans woman and a diasporic Chinese person who has always felt painfully disconnected from her cultural heritage, I have always felt the *cheongsam* was just out of my reach yet inexplicably far away—like a sense of ease with who I claim to be in the world. When I put on a *cheongsam* and look in the mirror, I can pretend, for a moment, that being a Chinese woman—whatever *that* means—is something that fits my body as beautifully and easily as actress Maggie Cheung's twenty-one vintage *cheongsam* in Wong Kar-wai's *In the Mood for Love*.

The problem is that most *cheongsam* are not easy to wear. Designed to adhere to patriarchal Chinese and European norms of female beauty, the figure-hugging design of the dress makes breathing difficult and free movement impossible; meant to emphasize (or demand) an hourglass silhouette, the *cheongsam* does not flatter a diverse range of body shapes.

Sitting in work meetings, surrounded by white cis women and struggling to breathe in my *cheongsam*, I have sometimes felt as stiff and repressed as a patriarch's ideal of women, as an outmoded feminist theory, as a colonizer's dream of the Orient. When I go to Chinatown to buy groceries or to eat my favourite salt fish fried rice, the stares I get from other Chinese people range from amused to outright hostile.

Even my white boyfriend is self-conscious about the attention and history that a *cheongsam* evokes: once, he told me he was nervous to be seen with me while I was dressed in *cheongsam* because people might think that he was pressuring me to wear it as part of some sort of Orientalist fantasy!

Strangely, all of this has made me more, instead of less, determined to find a way to make the *cheongsam* fit into my wardrobe and my life. For all its sexy, sultry glamour, I suspect that the *cheongsam* hides more than it reveals: The secret, perhaps, to who we are, as Chinese women scattered across geography and time. A path to who we wish to be.

The first dress I ever wore in public was a *cheongsam*. This was before I transitioned, before I grew out my hair, before I even called myself a woman. I wore it as part of a drag dance and spoken word performance. Unlike the demure cotton and wool *cheongsam* I wear today, this *cheongsam*, a gift from my best friend's Hong Kong–born mother, was made of bright red silk, the colour of pride and good fortune. It was adorned with dragons rendered in gold embroidery.

This dress was the beginning and the end: the beginning of my womanhood, the end of my boyhood. My Chinese past and my diasporic present. I still remember how it felt, the silk on my skin. My courage, my cowardice. How the dress became a part of me as I leaped and spun. As I sang. As I breathed fire.

growing

let us not speak
of what happened between us.
instead, let us speak
of what happened after:
my skin became a shroud
while the poison of your past
sank into my bones.
organs ossified, my liver on ice
electric shock signals
hardwired into the matrix
of nerves binding my brain, heart
and spine.
thoughts locked on loop, muscles flooded
with memory: trauma is the body
torn out of time.
no prayer had the power
to reach me then
no holy water could anoint this flesh.
faith is the connective tissue that binds us all
to the celestial bodies
of the universe.
faith is trust in the world
and mine was torn.
so when they came for me
eyes shiny, arms spread
i could not tell the difference
between the ones who came to help
and the ones came to feast.

i live in the earth now
stomach full of stones
my eyes full of dirt.
maggots wriggling
in the chambers of the heart.
but let us not speak
of what happened between us.
let us speak of the tree that is sprouting
from the centre of my throat.
of the luminescent fungi growing
on the inside of my skull.
of the flowers that still bloom
in every dead part
of me.

Where Did She Go?
A Trans Girl Ghost Story

This essay is a ghost story, a love letter, and a mystery.

I have loved so many mothers that I never got to know. They slipped through the cracks in the world as I was born, seconds too late, into woman-hood. Like fairy-tale princesses, they left traces behind, a shimmering trail of disjointed clues: pieces of art, political manifestos, grassroots community programs and services that they'd started from scratch on a shoestring budget. The evidence of their incredible lives, their fabulous gifts, their struggle, their survival shine brightly to trans girls who know where to look. The women themselves, however, are nowhere to be found.

When I was in my teens and early twenties, living in Montreal and still flirting with the idea of transition, there were already a handful of prominent trans women in North America—mostly artists, activists, and sex workers, though some others worked in the fashion industry or in health care. The prevailing media narratives around them were similar (if less politically nuanced) to those that surround trans women today, such as Janet Mock and Laverne Cox: stories of "gender revolution," societal boundary-pushing, tragic family histories yielding to triumphant reclamations of the body and soul.

As a writer and performer, I've noticed a tendency on the part of cisgender commentators to label any transgender-related phenomena as "new" or "groundbreaking." However, there have been famous (or, rather, infamous) trans people, particularly trans women, in every generation of Western media since at least 1930, when Lili Elbe scandalized Europe by undergoing one of the first gender reassignment surgeries, in Germany.

The public is fascinated by the stories of trans women, or rather, by what they imagine our stories to be: glamorous, scandalous, titillating, tragic. This narrative maintains itself in perpetuity, erasing both the inglorious mundanity of our actual lives as well as the cultural and historical lineages that contemporary trans feminine individuals stand to inherit. Trans women are always new and shocking, despite the fact that we appear across cultures globally throughout recorded history.

Yet every time a trans woman transitions in public—and in this era of social media and advanced surveillance culture, every trans woman transitions in public—she is immediately thrust into the role that our culture has made for her. She is a sexual sinner to conservatives, a tragic hero to liberals, and a revolutionary saint to leftist radicals. As a larger-than-life symbol, she stands alone. Symbols always stand alone.

I came of age as a trans girl in the early 2010s, in a cultural moment generally understood in the West to be the "tipping point" of the trans rights movement, accompanied by a kind of renaissance in trans cultural production. That is to say: we now had trans people on TV, (some of) whom were actually played by trans people. In my own field of writing and performance, transgender fiction and poetry finally began to break free of the sensationalized tell-all memoir genre to which we have historically been confined.

I was one of the first trans femmes in my cohort of queer friends to transition, a process made exponentially more public by my growing profile as an artist, writer, and general person-about-town (it's not that hard to become famous in the small pond of queer arts and culture). As a result, I frequently and quite unintentionally found myself in the position of "big sister" to many trans femmes, some of whom were older than me in years but coming out later in life. These relationships often took the form of brief, intense friendships in which the other person would ask for mentorship, with various degrees of explicitness.

To an emerging trans femme, mentorship is everything: we need mentors to teach us how to dress and apply makeup, how to carry ourselves, how to survive street violence and sexual harassment, how to do sex work (often the most reliable way for a trans woman to survive economically), and a thousand other things.

Being a "big sister" is often a fraught position. Although many of my "little sisters" remain among the most special relationships in my life, the responsibility of such a role is daunting, particularly when one is young and relatively new to transition oneself. I started mentoring people in my early twenties, and it wasn't really a choice—there was no one else to do it. There were so many things I didn't know that I wish I had, if only so that I could have passed them on sooner. So that I could have been a better and wiser older sister.

One question I have asked myself throughout my life is: Where were my big sisters? Where were my foremothers? Where were the older trans women, the accomplished trans women, the fierce survivor trans women that queer culture is so fond of mythologizing, in my life?

When I moved to Toronto in 2016, I had hoped to meet a particular trans woman artist whose body of work remains among the most challenging and brilliant in the world. Her star shone brightly while I lived in Montreal—she appeared in theatres and in newspapers, she wrote and performed and was written about constantly, it seemed. When I watched video clips of her, there was a magnetic glamour to her, a genius that was undeniable. She carved a path that continues to benefit trans women thinkers and artists today. I didn't presume that we would be friends, or that she would mentor me in any actual in-person way. I just thought that it would be inspiring or, I don't know, fulfilling in some way to stand in the same room as this incredible person. Trans community is small, and smaller when it comes to artists—I assumed that we would cross paths somehow, sooner or later. But by the time I arrived, she seemed to have abruptly disappeared from the public eye. Her performances and appearances, once so numerous, have—at least for the time being—ceased. Rumours about various misfortunes that might have befallen her swirled in response to casual inquiries such as, "Hey, what's that artist doing these days?" Respect for her privacy prevented me from inquiring further—just because her work was important to me didn't mean I had any right to knowledge about her actual life (something that "fans" of trans artists and media makers too often seem to forget).

But I still wonder: Where did she go?

The cisgender public labours under the assumption that trans women cannot be mothers because we are "unnatural" women, but the truth is that the trans woman as mother, nurturer, and protector is a pre-eminent archetype in queer cultural narratives.

The most famous examples of this archetype are none other than Marsha P. Johnson and Sylvia Rivera, a pair of racialized trans feminine individuals (many call them trans women today, but they are also on the record referring to themselves variously as drag queens and transvestites—terminology changes over time) who founded the STAR House for trans sex workers. These two heroines have acquired a practically sainted status in politicized queer communities for their radical politics and grassroots organizing work, in which they provided housing, care, and essentially, mothering to queer and trans young people.

Yet Marsha P. and Sylvia were not unique in their roles as trans mothers and mentors. Their work forms part of a frequently forgotten/invisibilized cultural tradition of trans women coming together—especially in the heavily racialized ballroom scenes of North America—as social outcasts and forming families based on mutual care, a tradition currently represented in the mainstream television show *Pose*. The heads of these families were older trans women whose greater experience and survival knowledge were a respected and essential part of queer survival. Such practices of informal, or "chosen" family (the level of choice is debatable, given its necessity for survival) are, I believe, alive and well in many places.

Yet although the trans mother of the house is very present as a historical legend in the urban queer communities that I grew up in, her actual embodied presence has been lacking in my life. Sisters, I have many, but mothers, I have none. For one thing, I have met very few trans women older than their forties, and those I have met tend (understandably) to decline the roles of "elder" and "mother," feeling ill-equipped or too young for the role.

There is a generational divide between older trans women who came of age in the 1990s and early 2000s, and those who transitioned after. This cultural gap is based in more than differences in perspective; rather, there is a literal lack of contact and communication between us. It is hard for young trans girls to find older trans women to be mother and mentor—hence, the emphasis contemporary trans culture places on transgender "possibility models" and celebrities.

One reason for this gulf is the impact of the AIDS crisis, the history of which tends to focus on gay men. Yet trans women, too, were implicated, their deaths often counted as part of the "men who have sex with men" category in social scientific research. Many trans women in the generation preceding mine simply died before we could meet them. Transphobic violence, which predominantly affects trans feminine sex workers, claimed still more.

Yet many trans women survived and continue to survive. Still, somehow they seem to disappear.

The legends of trans women and the work they have done to improve the living conditions of their sisters is littered throughout queer archives across the continent and the internet. In any major urban centre with a trans community, the work of a trans woman activist, artist, or community worker can be uncovered.

Toronto's robust LGBT non-profit sector, for example, now populated with literally dozens of LGBT-specific health and social service programs, was largely founded in response to the work of a small group of trans women.

Their names and contributions, their writing and artwork and activism are enshrined in queer archival and academic work. Younger trans activists and cultural producers refer to them often as forerunners and inspirations.

Yet the majority (there are always exceptions) of this cohort of trans women trailblazers seems to have departed from the public eye. Sometimes it seems that the higher a trans woman's public profile, the more totally and abruptly she disappears from public view. A friend of mine and I have semi-jokingly referred to this phenomenon as "passing through the veil"—like a mysterious ritual in a speculative fiction society composed almost entirely of young people.

You may have noticed that I'm not naming any trans women in this essay—except Marsha P. and Sylvia Rivera—though it's common practice to do so in queer writing as a way of crediting and honouring individuals. In this case, though, it seems more respectful to refrain from naming people and calling attention to them. People who have chosen to remove themselves from public visibility might rather stay unseen. In a time when so much of the queer rights movement is obsessed with visibility and representation, it occurs to me that trans women have rarely had the right to privacy in the first place.

Sex work and communities of sex workers have been present in my life for some time, as they are for many trans women. If you're a trans girl with trans feminine friends, you're probably, at most, two degrees of separation away from sex work. Like many industries based on providing services to humans, sex work can be both rewarding and harrowing. For trans women sex workers, however, the risks are exacerbated by transmisogyny and the stigma that surrounds our sexuality. This danger makes informal mentorships with more experienced trans women essential.

There was a time in my life when I was considering entering sex work to support myself financially and as a means of leaving a situation of precarity.

At that time, I could find no other trans women who were willing and able to mentor me in the field—I had many cis sex worker friends, but the worlds of trans and cis sex work are often radically different. So I did what millennials do best—I googled "how to be a trans woman sex worker" and was delighted to find an article with a twelve-point list on that very topic by an older trans woman that was both informative and personal.

I devoured that article. Here was hope. Here was guidance. Here was evidence that girls like me could survive and thrive in a field often literally equated to suicide by mainstream media. Hoping to find more pieces by the author, I googled her name, only to find that she had died by suicide just a year before.

There is something that happens to brilliant trans women. We don't seem to talk about it much. A story that keeps repeating itself: We burst into being; we give birth to ourselves. We burn like stars in the fight to survive. Like mayflies, we soar ever so briefly, then fall.

Over and over again, I come across the names of trans women who have come before, only to find that they have left this world—either by death or by suicide or by a madness that takes them so deep into themselves that they are lost to the rest of us.

My experience in trans women and sex work community has resulted in connections with many brilliant and revolutionary trans women. I do not know a single one who has not been seriously suicidal or in mental health crisis at some point in their lives—often more than once. Many, many times I have been woken up in the middle of the night by a phone call or a text message from a trans woman declaring her intent to die by suicide. On some terrible occasions, I have woken up to the news that a trans woman friend, or friend of a friend, has died.

On others, I have simply lost track of a trans woman acquaintance—fallen out of touch, watched from afar with some concern as her social media presence became more and more erratic, only to realize a few months or years down the road that nobody in our social circle knows where she has gone or what she is doing. At times, I have investigated further through the whisper networks of queer community and sex workers and their clients, finding only rumours that the trans woman I am searching for has "gone crazy."

I attribute this not to any inherent tendency toward mental illness in trans women but rather to the intense public scrutiny, violence, and other forms of trauma that infringe upon our lives. Trans women are brilliant; we shine because we have to in a world where are futures can seem overwhelmingly dark. I have always loved this fire that lives inside trans women.

But sometimes, I think I can hear them whispering to me. And I wonder: How long can it last? And how long until I disappear too?

I have had three very serious mental health breakdowns in my life so far. The first was in high school, the second was during my undergraduate degree, and the third was just last year. At each of those times, I was experiencing—to all outward appearances—material success. Last year, I published three critically praised books, won literary awards, was "famous" in queer community, and was also maintaining a demanding job in public sector clinical social work.

Beneath the surface of that success, however, I was in turmoil. My critically acclaimed books, and the heightened public profile that accompanied them, exposed me to stalkers and frequent emails from strangers asking for attention or free work. My "fame" in queer community resulted in jealousy and gossip, sometimes well meaning and sometimes malicious, which heightened my anxiety to the level of paranoia. These factors, combined with my position as a therapist to queer youth, meant that there was no respite in either my personal or professional life from narratives of trauma, enormous responsibility, and scrutiny.

The result was that I often felt as though I was going mad. In those terrible moments, it seemed as if there was no escape from the relentless projections of other people's desires, needs, traumas, fears. I was pushed to be perfect at all times, for all people—and the consequence of failure was punishment. It was suffocating. It was devastating.

When I was an adolescent, I used to long to be seen—I thought that to be seen was to be loved. I longed to be noticed, to be talked about, to be lusted after. Now, everyone sees me, and all I want is to be invisible. To be safe.

Trans women's bodies and behaviour endure intense social surveillance, both in and outside of queer communities. We carry the stigma of being, in the eyes of society, dangerous, perverted, mentally ill, deceptive, aberrant. On the flip side, trans women are also fetishized—not only sexually but also ideologically. To leftists and liberals, we are martyrs for social progress, cannon fodder for the cause. When I think of all those trans women activists and leaders who died or went mad before their time, I wonder: What if their well-being had been celebrated as much as their work? What if the communities that promoted their art, built social programs off their ideas, profited off their labour had been just as invested in preserving their lives and livelihoods?

If that had been the case, would I have a trans mother or big sister now?

This essay is a ghost story, a love letter, and a mystery.

All this time, I've been circling around the question: What happens to brilliant trans women who disappear? What happened to the women who might have been my mothers? We know part of the answer: Some of them died. Others went mad. Perhaps there are others who simply dropped out of the public eye—as much as any trans woman can—to try to live quieter, less visible lives.

I am haunted. All trans women are. Behind me stretches a line of ghosts—trans women, killed before their time by the hatred of a society that does not know how to love us. Perhaps this is why trans women's words are so powerful, in those rare moments when we are allowed to speak: we speak with the voices of those who have come before.

Perhaps this is why trans women dream so deeply—because we walk hand in hand with those in the next world.

When I ask myself the question: What happened to my mothers? I am really asking the questions: Where am I going? What will happen to me?

This world is a terrible and painful one to live in. I can hear the voices from another world calling my name. Sometimes I close my eyes and think, *It would be so very easy to go there*—whether through death or madness—and never, ever come back.

Dear sisters and mothers who came before: Someday I shall know you. In this world or the next.

But for now, something keeps me here: hope, I think, or maybe love. I wonder, can you have hope, or love, without faith? The faith that things will get better, that we will live long and happy lives, that some benevolent force in the universe will give us better endings? I think perhaps we can. What I hope for is to live as brilliantly as the mothers and sisters I've never met. I want to live for the ones who don't, for the ones who went before. I want to live as long and lovingly as I can.

what does it mean?

what does it mean
to be loved by a thing
that cannot see you?
how does it feel
to love a thing
that you cannot see?

Dear, Dear Life

One summer night a few years ago, my dear friend and soul sister Kama La Mackerel and I decided to take selfies atop the ruby-red stairs of the TKTS ticket seller booth in Times Square. We were in New York City for the weekend to perform at a fundraiser for the Audre Lorde Project, a non-profit organization that supports LGBTQ people of colour.

Hanging out in Times Square isn't exactly my idea of a good time—I like to think that I am a Sophisticated Lady who is above all that tourist cliché nonsense. But Kama, whose social media game is fierce beyond measure, was determined to get a photo of us on those stairs (#TWOCsistas #transgirlsinnyc #femme4femme #whathappensinnewyork). And what La Mackerel wants, La Mackerel *gets*.

Engulfed in the throng of tourists and street performers, we disappeared—just two more girls amid the crowd. This is unusual for us, because as trans women of colour, we are used to standing out wherever we go. To being pointed at, laughed at, cursed at. Threatened. Touched, grabbed, groped without our consent. To being both crudely and subtly degraded in the streets, on the subway, at work, in the bedrooms of our supposed lovers.

Sitting on that glowing red staircase under the artificial lights of the Times Square billboards, though, I felt totally and unexpectedly at peace with the universe. There, in the centre of the Western world, Kama and I (apparently not so sophisticated after all) clung to each other and shrieked and giggled and gawked like the small-town girls we are at heart.

"What are you thinking about?" she asked me, after we had both calmed down somewhat.

I opened my mouth to answer, but a lump caught in my throat. Tears prickled at the back of my eyes.

"I'm thinking about how far we've come," I said finally. "I'm thinking about how just a few years ago, I never thought I would be here. Or even alive. I never believed I could be this happy."

When you are a young trans girl of colour, you grow up knowing that you are marked for violence and death. Your classmates joke about hunting down and shooting people like you. It seems like almost every news item, book, movie, and TV show featuring a trans person ends with that person being rejected by their family, sexually assaulted, killed, or all three. Even the sympathetic portrayals seem to make us out to be victims to be pitied rather than heroes to be celebrated.

No one teaches you that you can be happy. No one shows you a vision of the future that you can see yourself in.

In 2014, *Time* magazine declared that society had reached a "trans tipping point"—a pivotal, triumphant moment for trans rights—spurring a surge of media attention on trans people, especially trans women. Yet the stories that are told about us in mainstream media remain, for the most part, painfully, terrifyingly limited: Dozens of articles about the trans body count of 2015. Stories about trans women coming out to enormous social backlash and violence, about trans women trapped in survival sex work, about trans women arrested and incarcerated for no reason other than being out in public.

It is vitally important to shed light on the oppression and suffering of trans women. I am glad that it is happening after generations of silence. But I also want to know: Where are the comics about trans lady robber barons? The magazine profiles about trans women making breakthroughs in STEM professions (and, yes, they do exist)? The Pulitzer Prize–winning novels portraying communities of trans women of colour living together and loving each other, despite the terrible odds?

More than ever, trans women of colour need be able to dream about ourselves as vibrant and powerful. As leading lives worth living.

For most of my life, I didn't know any trans people. The only trans folks I saw in the media were white and lived in worlds vastly different from my own existence as a Chinese kid growing up in an immigrant neighbourhood in Vancouver. I looked to the future and saw only fear, isolation, hardship.

When I told my parents that I was trans, they were even more afraid than I was. They grew up in a time when anti-Asian racism in North America was virulent and far less subtle than it is today. They knew what it meant to struggle endlessly to survive in a hostile world. They had spent their whole lives working to make sure that I would not have to live through that—and now, it seemed to them, I was throwing it all away.

Shortly after that less-than-ideal coming-out experience, I undertook my first suicide attempt. As my father drove me home from the hospital, he told me that "all of this"—my mental health, my gender identity—had to be kept a secret from our neighbours. Gossip spreads fast in the Chinese community, and he was worried that my mother's business would suffer for my "reputation."

So not only was I fated to live a nasty, brutish, and short life, but I would also bring ruin and shame upon my family. This, I learned, was what it means to be trans and of colour, a lesson that would take me years to unlearn.

Like my parents before me, I used to believe that the only way I could escape oppression and discrimination was by rising above it. If I could finish university, get a high-paying middle-class job, medically alter my body to look like a "normal" woman's, and find myself a nice white boyfriend, then I could be happy.

In other words, I thought that my salvation lay in making myself as non-trans as possible. I was a trans woman, but I did not want to be one of "those" trans women, as the media portrayed them: pitiful, ridiculous, unattractive creatures at the mercy of an unrelenting world.

Little by little, however, I came to one of the most important and powerful realizations of my entire life: trans women's happiness lies in loving other trans women.

When you are a young trans woman of colour, everyone tells you that the best you can hope for is to spend your life endlessly trying to win the grudging approval of others. They tell you that, at most, you may define yourself as a failed man, an artificial woman, an aberration of a human being. They tell you that if someone loves you, it is only in spite of your difference.

What they do not tell you is that you are far from alone. That there is a community of beautiful, brave, shade-throwing women just like (or at least, very much like) you.

Among your trans sisters, you are not the only one. You are not a freak to be pitied, a victim to be exploited, or a damsel in distress waiting to be saved. You are part of a fierce, fabulous family, a secret network of gender-bending women warriors helping each other to survive.

Everything changes when you know other trans women—when you have mentors, mothers, sisters, role models, guides. (And also, at times, frenemies. I think of them as role models of ways I do *not* want to be.)

It was a trans woman who gave me my first dress, taught me to apply makeup, showed me how to walk in heels. It was a trans woman who slipped me my first hormone pills, who brought me to the doctor who oversaw my medical transition. It was possibility models like Laverne Cox and Janet Mock who made me believe that I could be a writer.

My life is full of stories of incredible women, complicated women, ferocious women, tender women, all of us transgender and crackling with life. I know a trans girl who can make the most exquisite dresses. I know a trans woman who dances like a goddess of war. I know trans women who are models, actresses, activists, artists, scholars, and sex workers. Each of them teaches me how to laugh, how to be brave, despite knowing that someday I might be killed, the same way that Gwen Araujo or Kiesha Jenkins were—innocent girls, violently murdered for daring to live as trans.

"Brave" is such a strange and loaded word. Trans women hear it a lot these days. Well-meaning liberals call us brave all the time, because they are terrified of the thought of having to live like we do. They think that brave means always being alone, always needing to fight for space everywhere we go. Never knowing what tomorrow will bring.

Often, they are right. Too many trans people live and die alone.

But brave can also mean finding strength in numbers, finding your place among outcasts—solidarity and sisterhood. It can mean knowing that you may have to fight for the rest of your life, but you are never fighting alone.

When I was a social worker, I often met young trans women who wanted to transition but were well acquainted with the possible consequences of doing so: rejection by family, public discrimination, violence. One of them once asked me how I was able to live in my chosen gender presentation—if I was happy, and if I had any regrets.

For trans women, and perhaps for violently oppressed people in general, happiness has a different meaning from the one that is sold to us by Disney movies and the American Dream. "Happily ever after" is a concept that applies only to the wealthy and privileged.

We have to believe in happiness as something we can achieve not in some distant future where we are always safe and validated but in each moment that we continue to survive

When people like you are being murdered all the time, when gendered and racialized laws and social norms dictate almost every aspect of society, it is not possible to experience happiness as a state of permanent security. It is not possible to seek happiness in the approval of the majority of people around you, because no matter what you do, there will always be someone who perceives you as less than.

We are forced to redefine happiness as loving ourselves on our own terms.

This is the kind of happiness that is earned through acceptance of the ongoing battle. The kind of happiness that is only found at the centre of a whirlwind, in the arms of your community. And although I am not always able to find that feeling inside myself, the days that I can are more than enough to ensure that I have no regrets about my transition whatsoever.

When it comes to trans folks, people are always talking about gender *dysphoria*—dislike or hatred of the body or self. I want to talk about gender *euphoria*—the state of joy or delight in your being, your gender presentation.

For trans people, gender euphoria isn't a feeling that you can force yourself to have. It must be fought for, discovered, despite all the barriers in our way. It is something that is passed on, from one trans sister to another.

At some point in the past few years of my life, I found gender euphoria. I can't say exactly when or where. All I know is, these days, when I think about the future, I am so, so eager to find out what's next.

On the luminescent steps of the TKTS booth in Times Square, under the lights of billboards advertising Broadway shows and endless products, Kama and I traded stories: about her life growing up in Mauritius, learning to be queer in ways both similar to and totally different from my own path; about loving good and bad boyfriends; about navigating bureaucracy and health care as trans women.

We told each other, for the millionth time, how grateful we were to be in each other's lives.

And just as we fell silent, brimming with love, the crowd around us erupted in thunderous cheers and applause. For one crazy second, I thought they were applauding us, that the world had tilted off its axis and become a cheesy musical starring me and my friend.

Then I realized that a white, straight couple were the true centre of attention. The man was on one knee, a velvet box open in his outstretched palm to reveal the tiny star of a diamond ring. The women's hands flew to her mouth as tears trickled down her face.

"Yes," she sobbed, replete with the kind of happiness that girls like Kama and I might never know. "Yes."

And the man stood up and swept her off her feet as the tourists roared their approval and took a thousand photos to mark the occasion.

Standing among them, Kama and I were just two more girls amid the crowd. And although the bride-and-groom-to-be did not know it, did not even see us, we were laughing and crying along with them, for reasons both similar and radically different to theirs.

My sister and I stood on those glowing stairs to heaven in the centre of the world, and we held each other for dear, dear life.

for girls who are addicted to hurting themselves

never forget who you are
when the wind starts to blow in your rib cage
and the night starts to fall in your spine
when you look at your hands, so clean and so smooth
so gentle so pretty so brittle so sweet
like two dead branches of coral wrested
from the bottom of the sea
and placed on velvet in a glass box
and you wonder
who do these belong to?
remember

there was a time when you tore flesh
open with your nails
there was a time
when men feared your teeth
now, when people turn to you in wonder
as you claw your hair
and hurl yourself against windows
and ask, *have you gone crazy?*
you should take joy in knowing
that they are seeing you for the first time

it has been a long damn time
since you looked at yourself in the mirror
and saw the girl who could haunt someone's nightmares

it has been a long damn time
since you wrote a poem that could crack glass
when did you learn
that people preferred you this way?
when did you decide
that belonging with someone
else was better
than belonging to yourself?
remember

you are the girl who chose to wear red
who dreamed of fire, of flight
and went looking for the wolf in the woods
you are the girl who ran
between the trees, hair wild in the wind
you are the girl who stitched
a donkeyskin to her flesh
and haunted the countryside,
searching
for a life to call her own
remember

when you were sixteen in the hospital
locked in a glass box
and the policewoman who took you there
smiled and said, *you'll make a nice girl*
everyone loves a nice girl
even then you knew
that in your place
a nice girl would not have survived

somehow, you let yourself fall
into somebody else's dream
this tiny palace of crystal and soft fabrics
so nice
so sweet
so safe
you cut your shadow from your feet
and put it in a box so you could stay

still, your bones know: you are not this girl
you are not *his girl*
you are no one's girl
and you know how this story ends:

you must take your hands back
you must take your hair back
you must take your shadow back
you must take your teeth back

there is a moral to this tale, and you
were born to tell it
safe and free are not the same thing
living and alive are not the same thing

so tear your hair and blacken your eyes
sharpen your fangs, throw your bones
against mirrors and windows

break whatever you have to
take a shard of glass and write
an essay on your skin
that begins and ends
with the words:

never forget who you are

Acknowledgments

Of all the books I have written so far, this was by far the most difficult and daunting to publish. As such, I owe enormous thanks to everyone who helped along the way.

To Brian Lam, Shirarose Wilensky, Cynara Geissler, Oliver McPartlin, and the rest of the Arsenal Pulp Press team: thank you for believing in me and supporting me every step of the way.

To all the editors who worked with me on the many pieces in this book that have appeared in other publications in earlier forms.

To all the women and femmes whose work and writing in the area of transformative justice and healing justice has informed my thinking: Porpentine Charity Heartscape, Leah Lakshmi Piepzna-Samarasinha, Mia Mingus, adrienne maree brown, Morgan M Page, Sarah Schulman, and many others.

To Jake, my love, who listened to many a rant on every topic in this book.

To Kelly, Kama, Emily, and Kota, for being support through some of the most difficult moments of my life.

To Chanelle, Marty, and Jon, without whom I might not be around to see this book in the world.

To everyone I lost in the past few years to suicide, madness, violence, and trauma—I will always love you, in this world and in the next.

Photo: Rachel Woroner

KAI CHENG THOM is a writer, performer, and community healer based in Toronto, Treaty 13 territory. She is the winner of the 2017 Dayne Ogilvie Prize for Emerging LGBT Writers and a two-time Lambda Literary nominee. She has published widely, including the novel *Fierce Femmes and Notorious Liars: a Dangerous Trans Girl's Confabulous Memoir*, poetry collection *a place called No Homeland*, and children's book *From the Stars in the Sky to the Fish in the Sea*.